WHY DO WE HOPE?

IMAGES IN THE PSALMS

Daniel J. Harrington, s.j.

LITURGICAL PRESS

Collegeville, Minnesota

www.litpress.org

Excerpt from documents of the Second Vatican Council is from *Vatican Council II: The Basic Sixteen Documents*, by Austin Flannery, o.p. © 1996 (Costello Publishing Company, Inc.). Used with permission.

The Scripture quotations are from the *New Revised Standard Version Bible*, Catholic edition, © 1989 by the Division of Christian Education of the National Council of Churches of Christ in the U.S.A. Used with permission. All rights reserved.

Cover design by Monica Bokinskie.

1   2   3   4   5   6   7   8   9

Library of Congress Cataloging-in-Publication Data

Harrington, Daniel J.
  Why do we hope? : images in the Psalms / Daniel J. Harrington.
    p. cm.
  Includes index.
  ISBN-13: 978-0-8146-3085-3
    1. Bible. O.T. Psalms—Criticism, interpretation, etc.
  2. Hope—Biblical teaching.   I. Title.

  BS1430.6.H65H37 2008
  223'.206—dc22

                                             2007019773

CONTENTS

Prologue

THE PSALMS AS A
BOOK OF HOPE

For many Christians, Psalms is the most familiar book in the Old Testament. We read them, sing them, and pray them. But do we understand them? By that I mean to ask, Do we ever examine these texts from the literary, historical, and theological perspectives that modern biblical scholars use in their studies of the Psalms?

This volume has a double purpose. First, it seeks to initiate beginners (whether they be individual readers or members of a group) into the methods and concerns used in the close reading of these ancient texts. Second, it focuses on how the book of Psalms can contribute to our understanding and appreciation of the theme of hope. In an increasingly dangerous and often hopeless world we need to listen to what the Bible—our greatest spiritual resource, described in Vatican II's *Dei verbum* as "the soul of sacred theology"—might have to say on this topic.

This volume is a complement to my work, *What Are We Hoping For? New Testament Images* (Liturgical Press, 2006). It is perhaps more accurately described as a "prequel" to that book, since it tries to tell the story of the hopes of God's people before the time of the New Testament.

The hopes of the New Testament writers are clearly focused on the kingdom of heaven (Matthew), right relationship with God (Paul's letter to the Romans), and eternal life with God and the risen Christ in the New Jerusalem (John's book of Revelation). The hopes expressed in the Psalms are more diffuse and elemental. They are concerned with such basic realities as physical healing, finding security or refuge, and overcoming enemies. Many psalms assume a very attenuated version of life after death, and others direct their hopes to transient institutions like the Jerusalem Temple and the earthly kings of Judah and Israel. Nevertheless, the relatively tenuous hopes of the psalmists may often reflect better the turmoil of our own lives than do the neatly focused hopes of Matthew, Paul, and John. In this context we Christians today can read with profit the book of Psalms both as a mirror of our own experiences and as testimony to the varied hopes held by God's people prior to Jesus and the New Testament.

This volume presents close readings of forty psalms that contribute in various ways to our understanding and appreciation of the theme of hope. Each chapter consists of the quotation of a text in which the pertinent image appears, a literary analysis with particular attention to the psalm's literary form and structure, an explication of the text focusing on its use of images that may foster hope in some way, a concluding comment linking the image to the New Testament, and several questions for reflection and/or discussion.

THE BOOK OF PSALMS

The English word "psalm" derives from the Greek *psalmos*, which means "song of praise." The Hebrew title for the book is *Tehillim*, which also means "songs of praise." The term "psalter," which usually refers to the book of Psalms as a whole, comes from the Greek *psalterion* (a stringed instrument). The psalms are songs or poems. The book of Psalms in Jewish and Christian Bibles consists of 150 compositions of varying lengths. Some of them could easily be sung communally, while others (especially wisdom psalms) are more like individual meditations or poems.

The book of Psalms is traditionally divided into five "books" consisting of Psalms 1–41, 42–72, 73–89, 90–106, and 107–150, respectively. Each "book" ends with a blessing or doxology directed to God. The fivefold division is analogous to that in the first five books of the Old Testament, also known as the Pentateuch. There are even a few repetitions in the various books. Psalm 14 is the same as Psalm 53, and part of Psalm 40 appears in Psalm 70.

Our book of Psalms is clearly a collection of at least five collections or hymnbooks. Within the individual collections there are also blocks of psalms that point to smaller collections that may have been integrated into the larger five collections. The smaller collections include the psalms attributed to the Korahites (42–49, and 84–88) and to Asaph (73–83), as well as the psalms celebrating the kingship of God (93–99) and the "songs of ascents" (120–134). In short, the Old Testament book of Psalms is an anthology of songs and poems written at different periods in ancient Israel's history and brought together under circumstances generally unknown to us today.

Many psalms contain headings or superscriptions, as well as mysterious words like "Selah" in the main text. Some superscriptions connect the psalm to an event in David's life, while others associate the psalm with groups like the Korahites or with Asaph. Still others seem to refer to musical instruments or provide musical directions. In many cases, however, their meaning is now lost.

The numbering of the psalms and their verses causes many problems and much confusion. This book follows the now widely-used system in the New Revised Standard Version. In this system the superscriptions are in small print and not counted among the verses (though in the Hebrew tradition they are counted as verses). Moreover, the Greek Bible tradition counts the Hebrew Psalms 9–10 and 114–115 as single items and divides both Psalms 116 and 148 into two items. The Latin Vulgate (and the older Catholic translations based on it) follow the Greek numbering of the individual psalms. Most modern publications at least in English (including the New Revised Standard Version

and this book) follow the traditional Hebrew (Masoretic) numbering of the individual psalms.

The essays that follow in this volume are textual studies.
They are meant to be read alongside the biblical texts of the
individual psalms that they treat. As the base text I have used
the New Revised Standard Version, a modern translation (1989),
which is readily available in the English-speaking world. There
are many other good translations such as the New American
Bible, the New Jerusalem Bible, the Revised English Bible, the
New International Version, and so forth. Readers should be
forewarned, however, that there may be some discrepancies
between the translations, especially regarding the numbers of
the psalms and of the number of verses in them.

The 150 Hebrew compositions that make up our canonical
book of Psalms are songs and poems. The most obvious feature
of Hebrew poetry is called parallelism of members. That is, the
same point is made twice in slightly different language, whether
by means of synonymous or antithetical parallelism. The practice
reflects the oral-aural culture in which the psalms originated,
when people did not have the luxury of mass-produced written
texts before their eyes. While there are often different nuances
in the parallel statements, readers should not search too hard
for radically different meanings in them. In many psalms there
is a rhythmic quality to the language but little or no interest in
end-rhymes. There are, however, several acrostic poems in which
each verse or block of verses begins with each one of the twenty-
two letters in the Hebrew alphabet in succession. Psalm 119 is
the most extreme version of this convention

The language of Psalms has been described as open and
metaphorical. There are very few obvious references to concrete
historical events, thus rendering the psalms a poor source for
those who want to discover in them allusions to specific events
in ancient Israel's history. However, the general character of their
language has promoted their survival and flourishing for some
2,500 years. They may be compared (irreverently, I admit) to the
greeting cards sold in our stores today. Their wording is suffi-

ciently attractive and vague that they can express the sentiments of many different persons and so enjoy wide usage.

As songs and poems, the Psalms communicate imaginatively and emotionally. Most psalms rely on images, metaphors, and similes to make their points. Whatever arguments they make are developed mainly through their images and symbols. Moreover, they manage to express a wide range of emotions, including discouragement, rage, fear, gratitude, and joy.

The content and structure of most psalms are guided by their scripts or literary forms. Modern scholars have classified almost all 150 psalms into about ten or twelve different literary categories. The most prominent type is the lament (in individual and communal forms), in which the psalmist addresses God directly, complains about some sickness or other crisis, expresses trust in God's power to resolve the crisis, and asks God to do so. There are also thanksgivings (individual and communal), and songs of trust in God. Other categories are best understood with reference to their content. They may celebrate God's actions in creation or in Israel's history, the kingship of God, God's covenant with Israel, Mount Zion and the Jerusalem Temple, the gift of the law, the coronation of a king, and the institution of kingship itself. The wisdom psalms are more like instructions than songs. But in the final analysis almost all the psalms sing the praises of God in some way.

Many psalms are clearly associated with the worship and sacrifices carried out at the Jerusalem Temple. It seems that many laments and thanksgivings were composed especially to accompany the offering of material sacrifices (animals, crops, etc.). And the Zion hymns celebrate the Temple as God's dwelling place on earth. The book of Psalms is sometimes described as the hymnbook of the Jerusalem Temple. While that may be an exaggeration, it at least reminds us that many psalms arose out of the liturgical life of ancient Israel and should be read and used in that spirit today.

Some psalms are linked in their superscriptions with David and events in David's life. In the Jewish and Christian traditions

David has been regarded as the author of all or most of the psalms. David's reputation as a psalmist stems first of all from his playing the lyre and thus driving evil spirits away from King Saul (see 1 Sam 16:14-23). This reputation grew to the point that in one text among the Qumran scrolls it is said that David wrote 4,050 songs.

However, on the basis of modern critical analysis it appears that the book of Psalms is an anthology consisting of various compositions by multiple authors, ranging from as early as the tenth century to as late as the second century B.C.E. David is better viewed as the model and patron saint of psalmists than as the direct author of the whole book of Psalms. All the psalms were written in Hebrew and at least in the present form in the land of Israel. Many psalms (but not all) seem to have some connection with the Jerusalem Temple and its liturgies.

The psalms are now classic texts. That is, they have transcended their original historical settings and have been (and still are) prayed, recited, and sung all over the world. The genius of the psalms resides in their open and metaphorical language and in their ability to convey by images the message of hope in the God of Israel (the Father of our Lord Jesus Christ) to all kinds of peoples in many different times and places.

IMAGES OF HOPE IN THE PSALMS

Hope is not easy to define. A search of the dictionaries yields something like the following: Hope is a desire accompanied by the possibility of, or belief in, its realization. This definition indicates that hope has an object or focus, looks toward the future, and has a basis or ground in reality. Thomas Aquinas describes hope as "what is agreeable, future, arduous, and possible of attainment." The opposites of hope are despair (no hope at all) and presumption (someone else will take care of things).

In the Christian tradition, hope along with faith and love constitute the three theological virtues. They are "theological" in the sense that they have God (*theos* in Greek) as their origin, object, and ground. The ultimate hopes expressed in the New

Testament especially concern right relationship with God (justification), eternal life with God, and the future fullness of God's kingdom. These hopes are founded on faith in God (through Christ) and are expressed in love for God and others in the present.

In the Old Testament the hopes of ancient Israel as God's people are based on the person and promises of God. But the hopes are more varied and less focused on ultimate realities than in the New Testament. The people of God may hope for offspring and the promised land (as in the case of Abraham), Israel's goodness and greatness as a nation (Moses), an ideal king (like David), the peace of Jerusalem as the dwelling place of God (Psalms), Israel's return from exile (Second Isaiah), the restoration of God's people under a new covenant (Jer 31:31-34), or the vindication of the wise and righteous with the coming of God's kingdom (Daniel).

Along with the prophets, the psalms express the hopes of ancient Israel most vividly. For the psalmists, God is the source and primary object of hope. Their songs ask for healing, rescue, forgiveness, security, and many other things. They believe that only Yahweh, the God of Israel, can fulfill their hopes, and that only in God can they find refuge and stability in their lives. Since their hopes concern the future and involve the action of God, they often resort to figurative speech and metaphorical language. They employ images taken from their everyday life—sleeping, sheep, shadows, olive trees, darkness, and so on—to express what they most hope for from God. In addressing and speaking about God, they use various metaphors such as king, shepherd, rock, fortress, warrior, and so on. In attending to their images we today can learn (and adapt for ourselves) the hopes of our ancestors in faith and see how they perceived and approached God in prayer.

While Christian readers today will find much intellectual stimulation and spiritual profit in the images of hope in the psalms, we need also to recognize their limitations. For the psalmists, right relationship with God involved offering material sacrifices (animals, crops, etc.) at the Jerusalem Temple. They had no clear vision of eternal life with God as sharing in the divine glory. Rather, for them, life after death was to be a shadowy and dismal existence in the underworld, Sheol. And while the present dimensions of God's kingship were joyfully celebrated, there was little sense of a future, all-encompassing kingdom of God such as is envisioned in the Lord's Prayer (see Matt 6:9-13; Luke 11:2-4).

What the images of hope in the book of Psalms allow Christian readers today to see more clearly are the biblical dynamics of hope. The psalms are prayers to God but nevertheless are full of very human emotions, confusion, and even violence. They express the raw materials of hope and prayer, with frequent swings of mood and tone. Many psalms place their hopes in all-too-human (and now disappeared) institutions thought to represent God, such as kingship, the nation state, the Temple, the levitical priesthood, and material sacrifices.

Nevertheless, with their many and varied images of hope, the Psalms can help Christian readers today to get in touch with their own hopes, to express those hopes freely and boldly, and to look to God for refuge and help in their lives. The psalms are a very important part of our biblical and theological heritage. What Vatican II's Constitution on Divine Revelation says about all the books of the Old Testament applies very well to the Psalms: "These books, even though they contain matters which are imperfect and provisional, nevertheless contain authentic divine teaching" (*Dei verbum*, par. 15).

THIS BOOK

My aim in the forty essays on individual psalms that follow is to let the psalms speak for themselves, and to help readers today to approach them more intelligently and reverently. For the most part I interpret the biblical texts from the perspective of historical criticism. That means that I read the psalms as literary compositions (with attention to their words and images, structure, genre, etc.), in their ancient historical contexts (many have references to worship at the Jerusalem Temple), and with regard to their theological message for people in antiquity (and today). I also write as a Catholic biblical scholar who believes with the author of the letter to the Hebrews that "the word of God is living and active, sharper than any two-edged sword" (4:12). And so at the end of each essay there are brief remarks about how the image of hope in the psalm points to or is "fulfilled" in the person of Jesus or in early Christian life. Also included are questions for the reader's personal reflection or for group discussion.

It seems to me that the christological reading of the psalms is appropriate in a Christian interpretive context. Many Christian scholars today are content to leave the psalms back in antiquity as an interesting source for the history of Israelite religion. There are also more traditional Christian approaches to the psalms that take Jesus as their speaker throughout and as the embodiment or incarnation of the psalms. I want to follow a middle path between these two approaches. While respecting the psalms on their own terms, I also want to suggest that much in the psalms, especially their rich imagery of hope, comes alive when linked with the person of Jesus.

The theme of hope in the book of Psalms can be approached in various ways. When starting this project, my initial instinct was to treat the images of hope with reference to the literary categories into which the psalms fall (laments, thanksgivings, songs of praise, etc.). Another approach would be to gather all the references to hope and related themes in the psalms, and present a synthesis of what the texts say about the theme of hope. Still another approach would be to arrange the psalms of hope according to a theological pattern, a kind of "spiritual exercises" based on the psalms.

What finally seemed to me to be the most appropriate and effective approach has been to treat the images of hope in the context of the individual psalms as they appear in the traditional order of the book of Psalms. In real life hope takes place in many different settings, often in contexts of crisis and intense suffering. The psalms treated here reflect the often emotional and confused reality in which hope emerges. Moreover, images are generally polyvalent, that is, they can have more than one meaning. For example, water can be a symbol of both life and death. To grasp what an image means and to avoid letting it mean anything and everything (and therefore nothing), it is necessary to place each image of hope in a wider context. That is why I am inviting readers to work through specific texts and try to grasp the biblical dynamics of hope through the images found in the book of Psalms.

The male-oriented language in which the Hebrew texts of the psalms were composed reflects the androcentric culture of the ancient Near East and the grammar of Biblical Hebrew. I have generally followed the policy of the New Revised Standard Version in using inclusive language for humans and avoiding excessive male-oriented language for God. I have sometimes used the divine name "Yahweh" for the God of Israel, even though the NRSV uses LORD consistently where the Hebrew form YHWH appears. I often refer to "the psalmist" and use male pronouns when referring to him. The use of the singular form, however, should not give the impression that one man composed all the psalms. When referring to the compositions in general, I use "psalms," but when referring to the book as a whole or to specific compositions with their number, I use "Psalm(s)".

These short essays on forty psalms are intended for beginners in the formal study of the book of Psalms. They illustrate how biblical texts are interpreted today on the literary, historical, and theological levels. I hope that they may be used profitably by individuals and Bible study groups. The theme of hope lends itself to personal application and prayer. I suggest a form of spiritual reading (*lectio divina*) consisting of four steps: reading (What does the text say?), meditation (What does the text say to me?), prayer (What do I want to say to God on the basis of this text?), and action (What must I do in light of this text?). My hope is that readers will apply these techniques and questions to the 40 psalms covered in this book and to the remaining 110 psalms in the Bible.

THE PSALMS

1. THE TWO WAYS (PSALM 1)

> *"For the LORD watches over the way of the righteous,*
> *but the way of the wicked will perish."* (Ps 1:6)

The "way," and its many synonyms such as path, road, and street, is part of everyday experience for most of us. To get from home to work or school most of us need to travel by foot or vehicle along a way of some sort. When we start out, we usually have a goal or destination in mind, some other place where we hope to go and do something. In order to reach that destination, we need to move along a way or road. Our journey involves both a map (or set of directions) and a willingness to do what we have to do to reach our goal. In setting out on the way we hope that we will arrive safe and sound at our destination.

Psalm 1 is classified generally as a wisdom poem, and more specifically as a Torah psalm. It begins with a beatitude ("Happy are those who . . ."), a literary form found frequently in Jewish wisdom writings and in the gospels (see Matt 5:3-12 and Luke 6:20-23). A beatitude declares people to be happy, fortunate, or lucky on the basis of some attitude, virtue, or possession that they may have. A more literal rendering of Psalm 1:1 is in the singular ("Happy is the man who . . ."). However, its content is clearly applicable to men and women alike, and so the NRSV uses the plural forms to make the statement gender inclusive. Psalm 1 is called a Torah psalm (see also Pss 19 and 119) because in 1:2 the Torah or "law of the LORD" appears to serve as the roadmap along the way toward beatitude or happiness.

The image of the way appears first in the psalm's description of the righteous as those who do not "take the path that sinners tread" (1:1). It occurs again at the end as part of the summary statement that contrasts the ways of the righteous and of

3

the wicked (1:6). As a whole, Psalm 1 describes first the way of the righteous (1:1-3) and then the way of the wicked (1:4-5), and closes with an evaluation of the two ways (1:6). Another important pattern of images—the tree and the chaff—at the center of the psalm (1:3-4) serves to heighten the contrast between the two ways. The righteous are compared to a strong and flourishing tree planted (or transplanted) by a stream and so producing abundant leaves and fruits. The wicked, however, are like chaff, which are the coverings and other debris separated from grain in the process of threshing and then destroyed by fire (see Luke 3:17), and therefore an image of what is without substance and value.

The road map for the righteous as they make their way through life is the "law of the LORD," or the Torah. The most obvious sense of Torah is what is found in the first five books of the Bible, and more specifically the 613 commandments in the law of Moses. However, the term can also refer to specific decrees or decisions given by priests in the Temple and to the larger body of teachings contained in the Old Testament as a whole. In its context at the beginning of the book of Psalms the law of the Lord might also refer to the many and varied teachings presented in the 149 psalms that follow. The main point in Psalm 1 is that the righteous have divine guidance as they make their way through life and pursue the goal that they hope to reach.

By its position at the start of the Psalter, Psalm 1 introduces the dynamics of hope. Those who hope to be righteous or just in their dealings with God and other persons must choose between the two ways. While the way of sinners and scoffers leads nowhere good and ends in destruction (like "chaff"), the way of the righteous is productive and fruitful ("like trees planted by streams of water"), and leads to right relationship with God and personal happiness. The Lord not only supplies the map ("the law of the LORD") but also provides personal guidance along the route ("the LORD watches over the way of righteous").

Psalm 1 affirms that hope has a goal and that there is a way to it. It asserts that the realization of hope demands an initial decision between the two ways and a resolve to act in a manner appropriate to that decision. Having decided for the way of the righteous, one must learn that way and walk upon it. At the end of the Sermon on the Mount Jesus warns his hearers that the way that leads to life is hard and that few find it (Matt 7:14). However, in John 14:6 Jesus proclaims that in his person and teachings he is the way. And in Acts we find that early Christians frequently described their new movement as "the way." At the outset of the collection, Psalm 1 characterizes the journey of hope as involving a choice between the two ways and a decision to walk along the way of the righteous. We can be sure that God will supply both the directions and the personal loving care needed for those who choose the way of hope.

Questions: When did you choose the way of the righteous? What did you hope to find? What have you found?

2. THE ANOINTED (PSALM 2)

> *"The kings of the earth set themselves,*
> *and the rulers take counsel together,*
> *against the LORD and his anointed." (Ps 2:2)*

There are not many kings or queens in the world today. Those who remain are generally figureheads, occupied mainly in ceremonial or symbolic functions. Nevertheless, even these kings (and queens) are important, since they still embody the identity, history, and hopes of their peoples. In biblical times, however, kings were much more powerful. They often combined the political, military, and judicial powers that are now spread among various branches of government in modern democracies. In ancient Israel the king served as a very important image of hope.

Psalm 2 is classified as a royal or messianic psalm, since it pertains mainly to the king. The psalm may well have been composed as part of the ritual of the anointing and coronation of the king in ancient Israel (see also Psalm 110). At the heart of the psalm is the Lord's affirmation in 2:6 that he has chosen the king and set him up on his "holy hill" or Mount Zion, which was the site of both the Temple and the royal palace in ancient Jerusalem. In this context the king is affirmed not only as chosen by God but also as an instrument of God. The hope that the people have in the king is ultimately hope in the Lord.

Psalm 2 reads like the script for the coronation ceremony. It begins in verses 1-3 with a warning to subject peoples or groups not to take the change in rulers as a sign of weakness and so as the occasion for rebellion. They are reminded that the new king is also the Lord's anointed, just as his predecessors were, and so any revolt is bound to fail.

The heart of the psalm (2:4-9) is a series of oracles or definitive statements from the Lord God. In 2:4-6 God is said to speak from his heavenly court and to declare for all to hear that "I have set my king on Zion, my holy hill" (2:6). There can be no doubt that God stands behind the new king. In 2:7-9 the king claims to recount what he has heard from God, that he is now God's adopted son: "You are my son; today I have begotten you" (2:7). He also claims to have been assured of his sovereignty over other peoples and of the military means by which to enforce that sovereignty (2:8-9).

The psalm closes in 2:10-12 with another warning to those peoples or groups that might be tempted to rebel. Their rulers are counseled to continue to show allegiance to the Lord and his new king. By the symbolic actions of kissing the king's feet they are in effect demonstrating their subordination not only to the new king but also to the Lord whose king he is. If they refuse, they can expect to be punished by the Lord (whose "wrath is quickly kindled") through the agency of his newly anointed king.

In the context of the coronation ceremony the king emerges as an image of hope for the people of Israel. He is a symbol of their hope precisely because he was chosen by the God of Israel, and the Lord stands behind him. The king's relationship to God is so close that he can be called the "son" of God. Since the king is the agent or instrument of God, the plans and efforts by rebellious subordinates are doomed to failure.

Psalm 2 offers an ideal picture of the king in ancient Israel. Some may even describe it as royal propaganda. The ideology behind the psalm applies most obviously to David and Solomon, and perhaps to a few "good" later kings of Judah such as Hezekiah and Josiah. The books of Kings provide ample evidence for the less-than-ideal character and conduct of most kings in ancient Israel and Judah. The fact that Psalm 2 continued to hold up the king as an image of hope even after the institution of kingship had ended badly in 587 B.C.E. is a tribute to the power of hope among God's people.

Hope for an ideal king in the future is often called "messianism." The word "messiah" means "anointed one"; its Greek translation is *christos*. From Psalm 2:2 we learn that the king in ancient Israel was anointed as part of the coronation ceremony. Some Jews in Jesus' time still hoped for an ideal king who would combine the political, military, and judicial roles of the king, and so restore Israel to its past greatness and more. Early Christians so identified Jesus of Nazareth with this figure that "Messiah" or "Christ" began very soon to function as a surname for him ("Lord Jesus Christ").

Just as Psalm 1 began with a beatitude ("Happy are they who"), so Psalm 2 ends with another beatitude that declares "happy" all those who "take refuge" in the Lord (2:12). The term "refuge" and its synonyms is a recurrent and highly significant image of hope in the Psalms. A refuge is a place of safety and security. It is one of the things that the psalmists most hope for in their relationship with God. Psalm 2 reminds us that biblical hope is communal, that we hope not merely as isolated individuals but rather as the people of God, and that we do so through the agency of Jesus, the anointed of the Lord.

Questions: What do you imagine when you hear Jesus referred to as "Messiah" or "Christ"? What hopes (if any) do you associate with this image?

3. Sleeping (Psalm 3)

> *"I lie down and sleep; I wake again,*
> *for the* Lord *sustains me."* (Ps 3:5)

Sleep is necessary for good physical and psychological health. In the very act of going to sleep we let go of a certain amount of conscious control over our lives and the world around us. We trust that during our time of sleep life around us will go on as usual and that we will awaken refreshed and reenergized. There are, however, no guarantees. There could be an earthquake during the night, or we may die in our sleep. But we hope that when we do awaken, both we and the world around us will be pretty much the same as (or even better than) it was when we fell asleep. Falling asleep is an act of trust in the present and of hope for the future.

Psalm 3 is an individual lament. The psalmist's statement of trust in God in 3:5 uses the images of sleeping and awakening as an acknowledgment of dependence upon God. It outlines the whole process from lying down through going to sleep to waking up again. In this apparently natural process the psalmist finds the presence of God, and attributes his continuing existence and successful awakening to God's care: "the Lord sustains me." That personal experience of God's loving care is put forward as a reason to hope for rescue from present sufferings.

Almost half of the psalms in Book One of the Psalms (1–41) are individual laments. (For other lament psalms, see 4, 5, 6, 7, 9-10, 13, 14 (= 53), 17, 22, 25, 26, 27, 28, 31, 35, 38, 39, and 41.) Psalm 3 is an excellent example of the basic literary form of the lament. In almost all cases there are five elements: direct address to God, complaint, statement of trust in God, petition, and final word of hope or thanks. These five elements constitute the basic script of the individual lament. They may appear in different orders, and may be repeated in the course of the psalm.

Psalm 3 is directed to God ("O Lord"), thus making the psalm into a kind of conversation or dialogue rather than an objective description or narrative. The statements in the course of the poem are made to God rather than posited about God. By addressing God directly the psalmist hopes for a hearing and a response from God. The complaint is presented in general terms in 3:1-2. It concerns the many "foes" who have arisen against the speaker. What makes their attack so painful is their taunt that "there is no help for you in God." The superscription to Psalm 3 links it to David's flight from his son Absalom in 2 Samuel 15–16. While it is unlikely that this psalm was composed only for that specific occasion (since the language is so general), the heading is at least a good application or association of this psalm to David's plight. In fact, the genius of the lament psalms is the vagueness of their complaints. The "open" character of their language has allowed people for more than 2,500 years to identify their own situations with those of the psalmist precisely because the language is applicable to many persons and situations.

The initial statement of trust in 3:3-4 first celebrates God as the psalmist's protector ("a shield") and vindicator ("my glory, and the one who lifts up my head"), and affirms that in the past God has answered the psalmist's prayers. Then in 3:5 he uses the imagery of sleeping and waking to express his trust in God as the one who "sustains me." These reflections embolden the speaker to assert that on the basis of his knowledge and experience of God, he is now not afraid of ten thousand enemies. This element in the biblical laments is both an expression of the speaker's perception of God as the one who hears prayers and a subtle challenge to God to act favorably on his behalf. There is here a note of calling God to task or even "blackmailing" God, as if God's reputation and honor depend on a positive response to the psalmist's prayer.

In the petition (3:7) the psalmist calls on God to rise up and deliver him. The imagery accompanying his call may strike readers today as excessively violent. He asks God to strike his enemies on the cheek and break their teeth. While not acceptable or admirable to those who have been challenged to turn the other cheek (see Matt 5:39 and Luke 6:29), the rage expressed in the petition is at least understandable. Also, the speaker is asking God to do the punishing rather than acting as the avenger on his own. Moreover, the savagery of his request is an expression of the intense emotion that suffering persons often feel. And there is a certain symmetry with the complaint back in 3:2 that the enemies were saying, "there is no help for you in God." In other words, the punishment involving the mouth fits the offense that also involved the mouth.

The concluding word of hope in 3:8 affirms that deliverance belongs to the Lord, thus affirming that the basis of the psalmist's hope is God's proven ability to heal and save. It also asks a blessing on Israel as God's people, thus moving from the individual speaker to the community. Many laments (see, for example, 22:22-31) end on a note of vindication and thanksgiving, suggesting that the crisis has passed, the prayer has been heard and answered, and the speaker has offered a thanksgiving sacrifice in the Jerusalem Temple (as is suggested by the reference to the "holy hill" in 3:4).

The lament psalms remind us that in the midst of intense suffering we need hope more than ever. These psalms provide us with the words and images to express how badly we feel, help us to enter into uncensored dialogue with God, show us that we are not alone in our sufferings, and affirm our trust and hope in God's willingness to hear our cries and respond to them. For Jesus as one who makes the biblical laments his own, see the accounts of his prayer in Gethsemane (Matt 26:36-46; Mark 14:32-42; Luke 22:39-46) and his death (Matt 27:45-47; Mark 15:33-39; Luke 23:44-49).

The imagery of sleeping and waking at the center of Psalm 3 leads us to recall that the one whom we call upon in our sufferings has displayed loving care for us in the past and can be counted upon to do so in the present crisis. This psalm and the many other laments in the Psalter are in the final analysis hope-filled prayers based on our experience of the Lord as the one who sustains us in our sleeping and waking. For Jesus as the model of trusting sleep in the midst of chaos, see his behavior in the gospel accounts of the stilling of the storm (Matt 8:23-27; Mark 4:35-41; Luke 8:22-25).

Questions: Do you ever reflect on sleeping as an act of trust and hope? On whom or what do you base your hopes?

4. THE HUMAN PERSON (PSALM 8)

> *"Yet you have made them a little lower than God,*
> *and crowned them with glory and honor."* (Ps 8:5)

Humans are amazing creatures. While inferior to some other earthly creatures in size, strength, and speed, we have come to dominate planet Earth to a remarkable degree through our intelligence, ingenuity, and resilience. The business slogan that claims every problem is an opportunity explains much of our success. While there is no denying or ignoring the evils that humans have done and continue to do, the good that we have achieved in so many areas of our existence (agriculture, architecture, transportation, communication, medicine, technology, and so on) is manifest to us and a part of our daily lives. We are and should be a source of wonder to ourselves.

The very first chapter of the Bible celebrates humankind as the crown of God's creation. It affirms that we are made in the image and likeness of God, and granted dominion by God over the rest of creation (see Gen 1:26-31). Psalm 8 echoes these sentiments of Genesis 1 as it expresses wonder at the exalted place of humans in the divine plan of creation and salvation. The psalmist is so impressed at our abilities and achievements that he places us second only to God (and other divine beings) in the hierarchy of creation.

Psalm 8 is a hymn in praise both of God the Creator and of humankind as the high point in God's work of creation. The praise is addressed in 8:1 to God as "our Sovereign," thus reminding humans of their proper dependence and subordination before their Creator. It praises the "name" of the Lord as majestic (in the sense of awe-inspiring) in all the earth. The first and final verses say the same things and so provide a framework or inclusion in which the psalmist praises God's glory in the work of creation (8:2-3) and in humankind as the crown of creation (8:4-8).

The description of God's work of creation in 8:2-3 is somewhat obscure in the present form of the text (which still puzzles biblical scholars). It seems to evoke the ancient Near Eastern idea of creation as a struggle in which the supreme God overcomes and restrains the powers of chaos (the sea and death), and imposes order on the world. In this context the psalmist celebrates the Lord's ability to erect a barrier or bulwark upon his "foes" (the power of chaos). This achievement was so spectacular that even infants recognized it and praised the Lord for it (see Matt 21:16). Even though God resides in the heavens, we can glimpse God's glory by looking at the moon and stars above us.

As in Genesis 1, the crown of God's work of creation is the human person, the one whom we call "Adam," one of the Hebrew words for "human." The psalmist marvels in 8:4 that God should have taken such care for humankind. Here the inclusive language of the NSRV obscures the play on the singular forms "man" and "son of man." In 8:5 the psalmist observes that the Lord has made humans "a little lower than God." Here the Hebrew term for God is *elohim*, a plural form which can be translated as "gods" or "divine beings." In Jewish and Christian theology these figures are traditionally identified as angels. In the earlier ancient Near Eastern context of Psalm 8, they were more likely understood as the gods or divine beings who constituted the council of the gods at which Yahweh ("the LORD" in the Psalms), the God of Israel, presided. The basic point is that in the order of creation humans stand second only to the divine beings (including the Lord).

In 8:6-8 the psalmist again echoes the language of Genesis 1:26-31 in attributing "dominion" to humans over the other orders of creation on the land (sheep and oxen), in the air (birds), and in the sea (fish). With dominion, of course, comes responsibility and stewardship. God the Creator and Lord has so much confidence in humans as to make us stewards of all the earth. Dominion is not an excuse to plunder the riches of the earth. Rather, humans have as their divinely appointed task caring for all the creatures of the earth. The psalm ends in 8:9 as it began in 8:1 by recognizing God's sovereignty and praising God's name.

God's special care for humankind as described in Psalm 8 is an important reason for hope. For all the evil that we do, we can look to Genesis 3 (original sin and the fall) for a rationale. For all the good that we do, Psalm 8 (and Gen 1:26-31) provides an explanation. The letter to the Hebrews (in 2:5-9) interprets the praise of humankind in Psalm 8:4-5 not as describing humans in general but rather as referring specifically to Jesus in his incarnation, and in his saving death and resurrection. It identifies Jesus as the "son of man" par excellence, interprets the Incarnation and Passion as his being lower than the angels for a while, and understands the Resurrection as his being crowned with honor and glory. This christological reading of Psalm 8 reminds us that the ultimate basis of Christian hope resides not merely in our human intelligence, ingenuity, and resilience, but also and especially in Jesus the God-man and in the paschal mystery of his life, death, and resurrection.

Questions: What human achievements have been sources of hope for you? Are there moments when you have been especially proud to be a human being? How do you react to the christological reading of Psalm 8 in Hebrews 2?

5. THE HOLY HILL (PSALM 15)

> *"O LORD, who may abide in your tent?*
> *Who may dwell on your holy hill?"* (Ps 15:1)

Mountains have always fascinated and attracted humans. Some people climb mountains out of curiosity to find out what is on top or on the other side, or to prove their ingenuity and stamina. For many there is also a religious dimension in which the mountain represents symbolically a closeness to the divine presence. In Greek religion Mount Olympus was regarded as the abode of the gods. In Hebrew religion Moses received the Law or Torah on Mount Sinai, and the central shrine was built on Mount Zion.

The expression "holy hill" in the psalms refers generally to the Temple built on Mount Zion in Jerusalem by Solomon in the early tenth century B.C.E. and rebuilt after the return from exile in the early sixth century B.C.E. The adjective "holy" (*qadosh* in Hebrew) evokes images of the separation from the common or profane that mountains provide. To come to God's holy hill in Jerusalem expresses the hope that there the God of Israel will be encountered in a special way. To make this hope into a reality one must undertake the arduous journey up to the city of Jerusalem (which is in a mountainous area) and enter the precincts of the Temple there. Those who make such a journey hope to find God on the holy hill.

Psalm 15 is often described as reflecting a liturgy of entrance into the Temple compound. In this scenario the pilgrims first ask God in 15:1 about the qualifications that they need to gain entrance to God's holy hill. The parallel term "tent" refers to the tabernacle or portable shrine that the ancient Israelites first carried around in their wanderings in the wilderness and then transported from place to place in the Holy Land before the Jerusalem Temple was built.

Solomon's Temple in Jerusalem was regarded as the successor to the tabernacle with its ark of the covenant. The installation of the ark on Mount Zion symbolized the stable presence of God there and made the Jerusalem Temple complex into God's holy hill. By asking questions about abiding in God's tent and dwelling on God's holy hill, the pilgrims make clear that in this place they hoped to find God and to experience God in a special way because God was present there in a special way. Many of the psalms reflect their use in connection with rituals carried out at the Temple.

The rest of Psalm 15 (vv. 2-5) records the answer that the pilgrims receive from God, most likely through a priest or other cultic official. The qualifications demanded for the pilgrims to enter God's holy hill do not involve observing rules of ritual purity or offering material sacrifices (though these were probably assumed). Rather, Psalm 15 lists the moral characteristics and behaviors that pilgrims must manifest in order to enter and remain at least for a time at the holy hill where God dwells in a special way.

What is expected of visitors to the holy hill is stated first of all in 15:2 in terms of what we might call moral integrity: walking or living blamelessly, doing what is right, and speaking the truth. Furthermore, they are expected in 15:3 to behave properly with regard to their neighbors by avoiding slander, doing no evil to them, and not reproaching them. According to 15:4a, they are in general to despise the wicked and honor those who fear the Lord. Finally, in the legal and economic areas of life (15:4b-5a), they are to carry out their oaths and promises even when this is difficult for them, not to loan money at interest, and not to take bribes so as to convict the innocent. The summary in 15:5b affirms that those who conduct themselves in these ways may gain admittance to the holy hill and fulfill their hopes of encountering God there.

Mountains in general and Jerusalem's holy hill in particular are images of hope. We approach them in the hope of coming into contact with the transcendent, meeting God halfway as it were, and enjoying a special closeness to the divine. Psalm 15 reminds us that the search for intense religious experience involves the cultivation of virtues, attitudes, and conduct that are appropriate to encountering the all Holy One.

There are holy hills in the gospels besides the Jerusalem Temple. Jesus delivers the Sermon on the Mount in Matthew 5–7, is transfigured on a high mountain, dies near the Temple Mount in Jerusalem, and commissions his disciples to carry on his movement on a mountain in Galilee (Matt 28:16-20). In the spirit of Psalm 15:2-5, Jesus in Matthew 5:23-24 urges his followers to be reconciled with others before offering their sacrifices at the Jerusalem Temple. And just as Psalm 15:2-5 lays down the moral entrance requirements for admission to the holy hill, so with the Beatitudes in Matthew 5:3-12 Jesus sketches out what is required for entering the kingdom of heaven.

In his dialogue with the Samaritan woman, Jesus promises that in the future God will be worshiped no longer exclusively at the holy hills of Samaria and Jerusalem but rather everywhere "in spirit and truth" (see John 4:21-24). In the mystery of the Incarnation, God has come down from the mountain and made the divine presence available to all in and through Jesus as Emmanuel ("God with us"). While the holy hill remains an image of hope, the longings and desires that it expresses are now more accessible through Jesus as the Word of God who became human and dwelt among us.

Questions: What feelings have you experienced on a mountain top? What do you hope for on entering a great cathedral? Do these experiences affect how you act?

6. THE SUN (PSALM 19)

> *"Its rising is from the ends of the heavens,*
> *and its circuit to the end of them;*
> *and nothing is hid from its heat."* (Ps 19:6)

Where I have lived most of my life (near Boston, MA), we have a large number of cloudy and rainy (and snowy) days. For us the sun is a welcome sight, and gives us hope that more good days will follow. The world around us looks better when the sun is out at full strength. The sun warms us up, makes the grass and plants grow, and illumines all our surroundings. For New Englanders at least (and for most people in our world), the sun is a sign of hope, and we feel better for its presence and look forward to more of it.

The first part of Psalm 19 reflects on how God's glory is revealed in the cosmos, especially in the sun. As people of their times, the psalmist and his audience supposed that the sun makes its orbit around the earth while the earth stands still. Although we moderns know otherwise, most of us instinctively still operate out of the old common-sense cosmology. We not only understand the imagery of Psalm 19 but also need to remind ourselves that in this case the scientific reality differs from the appearances.

Psalm 19 combines several formal categories. It begins with what looks like a creation hymn (19:1-6), moves into a Torah psalm (19:7-10), and ends with a petition for forgiveness and guidance (19:11-14). While some scholars have suggested that three short pieces have been joined together, there is nevertheless a logic that unites the parts. Just as the sun illumines our world, so the Torah (or God's revelation) illumines our human existence.

The first part (19:1-6) describes the cosmos as a witness to the glory of God. The heavens above us point to their creator, and day and night help us to know God's glory in many ways. Even though these creations do not use our words to communicate, their message is intelligible to all who are willing to understand it. There is an omnipotent, omniscient, and beneficent God behind the cosmos.

The sun is the most prominent and important among the heavenly bodies, at least for inhabitants of the earth. So central has the sun been in human history that in many cultures the sun has been deified or at least assigned to a special sun god. Psalm 19, however, makes it clear that the sun is the work of the supreme God (*El* in Hebrew) and is thus subordinate to that supreme God.

In the psalmist's conception of the universe God has assigned a tent for the sun, and at his command the sun makes its circuit around the earth during the course of the day. In 19:5 the psalmist compares the sun's emergence from its tent first to a bridegroom emerging from his wedding chamber and then to a strong man running his course with joy. Both comparisons convey ideas of strength and happiness, as befits the sun.

As the sun illumines the universe, so God's revelation illumines human existence. That is the implication of the Torah section (19:7-10) when joined to the creation section (19:1-6). In

19:7-9 there are six synonyms for divine revelation contained in the Torah: "law," "decrees," "precepts," "commandment," "fear of the LORD," and "ordinances." See Psalm 119 for an even more grandiose application of this device. In the first three cases there are references to three benefits of the divine revelation. It revives the soul, makes the simple wise, and causes the heart to rejoice. Next there are three characterizations of the revelation itself. It is "clear," "pure," and "true." Then in 19:10 there are two comparisons designed to emphasize how attractive and important the Torah is. It is more desirable than gold and sweeter than honey. Just as the sun reveals God's glory in creation, so the Torah reveals God's wisdom in human existence.

The concluding section (19:11-14) applies the basic insights of the first two parts to the speaker. The Hebrew verb *zahar* in 19:11, which is translated by the NRSV as "warned," can also be rendered as "illumined." Here it is applied to the illumination gained from God's wisdom and the rewards obtained by observing it. Next in 19:12 the psalmist asks for forgiveness for his "hidden faults," which are most likely unconscious infractions of some rules in the Torah. Then in 19:13 he seeks protection from the insolent who might lead him astray. The psalm ends in 19:14 with a prayer that the speaker's words might be acceptable to God and with an affirmation of confidence and trust in God as "my rock and my redeemer."

For Christians, Jesus is "the reflection of God's glory" (Heb 1:3) and the authoritative interpreter of the Torah (Matt 5:17-20). In the episode of the Transfiguration (Mark 9:2-8; and parallel accounts), Jesus combines the two great themes of Psalm 19. The disciples experience him in great brilliance and enjoy a preview of his resurrected glory. They see Moses and Elijah, symbols of the Torah and the prophets, conversing with Jesus and as somehow subordinate to him. Finally Jesus is identified by the voice from heaven as the Son of God, and we are told to "listen to him" (9:7). In his transfiguration Jesus appears as the actualization and personification of Psalm 19. As such he deserves the title Sun of Righteousness bestowed on him in some early Christian circles. That title is based on Malachi 4:2: "But for you who revere my name the sun of righteousness shall rise, with healing in its wings."

Questions: What hopes do you attach to sunrise and sunset? How does the divine revelation expressed in nature and in Scripture illumine your life?

7. THE INFANT (PSALM 22)

> *"Yet it was you who took me from the womb;*
> *you kept me safe on my mother's breast."* (Ps 22:9)

When and where do we learn to hope? Psychologists tell us that we first learn to hope at our mother's breast. As infants just after birth we instinctively seek nourishment and personal contact. And we find these human necessities with our mothers. In doing so we enjoy our first experiences of hope fulfilled, and throughout our lives we build upon these primal experiences of desire and its fulfillment. Whether those who are deprived of hope as infants become hopeless as adults, we can leave to the psychiatrists to decide. But most humans learn the dynamics of hope and trust at their mother's breast. We learn about hope at a very early age.

Psalm 22 is an individual lament. It is perhaps the longest and richest of the many laments contained in the Psalter. It is especially famous because its first words ("My God, my God, why have you forsaken me?") are the last words of Jesus according to Mark 15:34 and Matthew 27:46. One of the lesser noted images in Psalm 22 is that of the infant at its mother's breast in verses 9-10. This image of hope is part of the psalmist's declaration of trust and hope in God in the midst of intense personal suffering.

Psalm 22 contains in abundance all the elements of the biblical laments: direct address to God, complaint, declaration of trust, petition, and celebration of deliverance. The first eleven verses consist of alternating complaints (22:1-2, 6-8) and declarations of trust (22:3-5, 9-11). After the address ("My God, my God"), the psalmist complains in verses 1-2 about God's apparent disregard of him and refusal to hear his prayers. The first declaration of trust (22:3-5) focuses on the holiness of God and God's willingness in the past to answer the pleas of Israel, most likely in the exodus from Egypt. The second complaint (22:6-8) is concerned especially with the dishonor and shame that the psalmist feels in his sufferings ("I am a worm, and not human") and the taunts that his enemies are throwing at him. The second declaration of trust (22:9-11) features the image of the infant at its mother's breast. Here the psalmist points to his own personal experience, not that of the whole people or an event in the distant past. What is most striking is the stress on God's role in the mother-child relationship as the primal experience of hope ("it was you . . . On you I was cast"), thus taking it out of the psychological domain and placing it in a theological context. The psalmist points to his own first experiences of trust and hope fulfilled as a basis for his hoping that the present crisis will pass and that he will be rescued and vindicated.

The extended complaint in 22:12-18 features various animal images to describe the psalmist's tormentors (bulls, lions, dogs) and references to the parts of the body in pain (bones, heart, mouth, tongue, hands, feet) to dramatize his physical sufferings. The petition in 22:19-21 ("O my help, come quickly to my aid!") is apparently successful, since the rest of the psalm (22:22-31) is a celebration of what the psalmist believes that God has done on his behalf.

It is possible that the second part of Psalm 22 was originally part of a thanksgiving sacrifice carried out at the Jerusalem Temple. The speaker testifies in public about what God has accomplished for him, refers to fulfilling his vows (probably to offer sacrifices), and invites the poor to share in his good fortune by eating the leftovers from the sacrificial meal. Then he enlarges the scope of the celebration by inviting the whole world—past, present, and future—to join him in confessing that "he [God] has done it" (22:31). The lament psalm ends on a note of vindication and celebration. What the psalmist hoped for—rescue and vindication—has come to pass. The trust in God learned from infancy has been justified.

Psalm 22 is essential for understanding not only the last words of Jesus but also the mockery of him by those standing near the cross (Ps 22:7, 13 = Mark 15:29; Matt 27:29, 39) and the casting of lots for his garments (Ps 22:18 = Mark 15:24; Matt 27:35; Luke 23:34). As early Christians tried to make sense out of what had happened to their beloved teacher and hero, they turned to Psalm 22 (and the Servant figure in Isa 53) and found there material that gave them an entry point into the mystery of the cross.

To understand Jesus' death properly as it is presented in the gospels, it is important to read all of Psalm 22. To imagine on the basis of the opening words that Jesus despaired at the moment of his death runs counter to everything that the gospels say about Jesus. Rather, Mark and Matthew invite us to understand Jesus' death in terms of the whole of Psalm 22, with its descriptions of intense suffering and its declarations of trust in God as well as its concluding proclamation of rescue from death and vindication. Psalm 22 points not only to Jesus' death but also to his resurrection.

Questions: What about infants makes them signs of trust and hope? Is Psalm 22 a psalm of despair or of hope? Why is Psalm 22 appropriate for the Good Friday liturgy?

8. The Shepherd (Psalm 23)

> *"The* Lord *is my shepherd, I shall not want."* (Ps 23:1)

For most of us today, shepherds are not part of our daily lives. Nevertheless, we can easily understand and relate to the biblical images of sheep and shepherds. The shepherd knows his flock, leads them, and cares for them. In the ancient Near East the image of the shepherd was often applied to kings and other leaders. The image lives on today in religious circles where the leader of a church community is often called its "pastor" (from the Latin word *pastor*, for shepherd).

Psalm 23 is the best known and most popular of the 150 psalms. It is a psalm of trust, and applies the image of the shepherd to God. Many people recite it in times of danger or stress, and find in it renewed confidence and direction. It provides hope insofar as it reminds us that even in danger and confusion God knows us, leads us, and cares for us. With God as our shepherd we can hope to reach our goal.

The image of God as a shepherd is developed in detail in 23:1-4. Then in 23:5 the imagery switches to that of God as host of a grand banquet. The final verse (23:6) explains what we hope for and how we may obtain it.

Unlike most of us today, the people who first heard or read Psalm 23 had everyday experiences of sheep and shepherds. For the psalmist to identify the Lord as their shepherd evoked many positive associations in them. These associations are spelled out in Psalm 23:1-4. Of course, the Lord is no ordinary human shepherd. He does only the best things that good shepherds do, and does them even better.

With the Lord as my shepherd, I shall not want. This is the most fundamental and memorable affirmation in Psalm 23. No matter what obstacles and dangers occur, I can trust that God knows me, leads me, and cares for me. I will not be left alone and abandoned. This assurance makes hope possible and even reasonable.

The good shepherd provides abundant food and safe drinking water for his sheep. He cares for their basic material needs in "green pastures" (for eating) and by "still waters" (for drinking). The good shepherd leads the sheep in "right paths" because he knows the terrain and is able to keep his sheep on track, safe, and sound. He does so not only out of care for his sheep but also "for his name's sake," that is, so that others may recognize what a good shepherd the God of Israel really is. This latter point is an example of the frequent biblical challenges to the God of Israel to act in such a way that other nations may recognize and respect his honor and good name.

In 23:4 the psalmist evokes the especially frightening experience of walking through "the darkest valley" (or literally, "the valley of the shadow of death"). The idea is that with the Lord as our shepherd we can overcome even our greatest fears. The reason for this trust and confidence is the Lord's presence with us. The shepherd's rod and staff not only keep his sheep in line but also protect them against predatory animals. The imagery of the Lord as our shepherd helps us to understand why we can be people of hope in the first place.

In 23:5 the imagery changes to that of a grand banquet with the Lord serving as its host. Whereas the shepherd imagery describes the journey of hope, the banquet imagery evokes the goal or destination of that journey. The Lord is the one who prepares and furnishes the banquet. An added pleasure is that the psalmist's enemies have to watch the banquet from a distance. Meanwhile, the psalmist is treated as an honored guest (he is anointed) and has plenty to eat and drink (his cup overflows).

What the psalmist hopes for is summarized in 23:6. He hopes that God's loving care ("goodness and mercy") will guide him along through life, and that he will always dwell in the presence of God. The "house of the LORD" may refer to the Jerusalem Temple, the usual meaning of the expression in the Psalms. But here it may also have the wider sense of the land of Israel or the land of the living in general (as opposed to Sheol as the abode of the dead).

In the parable of the Lost Sheep in Matthew 18:10-14 and Luke 15:4-7 Jesus uses the image of the shepherd who actively seeks out his sheep as a defense or explanation for his own ministry to the marginal persons in his society. In John 10:1-18 Jesus identifies himself as the Good Shepherd who knows, leads, and cares for his flock. So great is his devotion to his flock that Jesus the Good Shepherd willingly lays down his life on their behalf (see John 10:15-18). He does so in order that they may enjoy the banquet that takes place in the kingdom of God and at which he as the Messiah (the anointed one) presides.

Questions: What is there about shepherds that makes them signs of hope? How does the banquet image function in the psalm? Do you ever pray Psalm 23 in times of stress or fear?

9. THUNDER (PSALM 29)

> *"The voice of the LORD is over the waters;*
> *the God of glory thunders,*
> *the LORD, over mighty waters."* (Ps 29:3)

In most of us there is an ambivalence about thunder. On the one hand, we know that thunder is often accompanied by lightning and torrential rains, and so we may legitimately fear for our safety. On the other hand, we may perceive in such a storm a display of the power and majesty of nature (and of God). More-over, thunderstorms usually do not last long, and so we may hope for the quick return of more tranquil weather.

The climate of the Holy Land is quite predictable. There is a rainy season from October to April, while the other months are dry. The rains are essential for the success of the agricultural cycle, and behind the traditional Jewish festal calendar is the cycle of harvests in the land of Canaan. In this context the beginning of the rainy season with its occasional thunderstorms is welcomed as a sign of hope for the harvests of the future.

Psalm 29 affirms the kingship or sovereignty of the God of Israel with the imagery of a thunderstorm. After inviting other members of the heavenly court to acknowledge the sovereignty of Yahweh (29:1-2), it celebrates that sovereignty in terms of seven thunderclaps interpreted as the "voice of the LORD" (29:3-9), and closes with a recognition of Yahweh as Lord over heaven and earth (29:10-11).

The invitation to recognize Yahweh's sovereignty (29:1-2) presupposes the ancient Near Eastern image of the heavenly realm as the council of the gods. Some scholars even have suggested that Psalm 29 is the Jewish adaptation of what was originally a hymn to the Canaanite god Baal. Here the "heavenly beings" (literally, the "son of the gods") are summoned to acknowledge the glory and strength of Yahweh, and to bow down before him in worship. Later Jewish and early Christian interpreters identified the heavenly beings as angels. This development reflects the trend toward a stricter monotheism than may have been supposed in the composition of Psalm 29. But the point of Psalm 29 in its present form is that Yahweh the God of Israel (and not Baal or any other god) is supreme in the council of heavenly beings.

In the cosmology of antiquity the gods or heavenly beings dwelt above the earth. In this framework thunder was often understood as a communication from the heavenly realm to earth. There even developed a "science" (brontology) for the interpretation of thunderclaps. In Psalm 29:3-9 the seven references to the "voice of the Lord" are regarded as signs of the power of Yahweh the supreme God, and the thunderstorm is considered to be a theophany, that is, a manifestation of the glory of God.

The description of the seven thunders tracks a storm moving from west to east, that is, from the Mediterranean Sea to over the lands of the ancient Near East. Out over the waters (29:3-4) the thunder points to the glory, power, and majesty of God. Over the land (29:5-9) the thunders with the accompanying lightning and rain are powerful enough to break the mighty cedars of Lebanon and to shake the earth. They signify the power of heaven over earth. The proper human response to the display of divine power in thunder is awe, and then the recognition and acknowledgement of the sovereignty of the Lord of all. And so on earth, in the Temple (presumably the Jerusalem Temple), all say, "Glory!" (29:9). The seven thunders point to the powerful and glorious God as the primary reason for our hope.

Psalm 29 ends with an affirmation of the kingship of Yahweh in heaven and on earth. In 29:10 he is pictured as enthroned above the flood (and so in control of it) as king forever. In 29:11

the psalmist asks God to give strength to his people Israel and to bless his people with peace.

For the psalmist and other ancient Near Eastern peoples, a thunderstorm could be interpreted as a sign of the power and glory of God. In that context a thunderclap might be identified as the "voice of the LORD." The imagery of Psalm 29 may stand behind the gospel accounts of Jesus' baptism and transfiguration. There (see Mark 1:11 and 9:7) a mysterious "voice" from heaven identifies Jesus as God's beloved Son and orders the persons around him to "listen to him."

Thunderstorms are ambivalent experiences. Despite their obvious dangers, however, they can be viewed as manifestations of God's majesty, and so as occasions for hope in the one who sits enthroned above the flood as king forever. Perhaps we need to listen more carefully for the voice of the Lord in our lives.

Questions: How do you regard thunderstorms? Can you imagine in a powerful storm anything positive or hopeful? Can you ever hear the voice of God in them?

10. THANK YOU! (PSALM 30)

> *"Sing praises to the LORD, O you his faithful ones,*
> *and gives thanks to his holy name."* (Ps 30:4)

It is considered polite behavior to say "thank you" when someone performs a service for us, gives us something, or does a favor on our behalf. Most of our "thank yous" are formulaic. Sometimes we are not sure what we mean to say or whether our benefactor even hears us. However, there are occasions when we recognize that what has been done for us has been more than ordinarily significant in our lives. Then we want a more formal setting at which to express our gratitude, and we want our friends to join in our thanksgiving. We want to say "thank you" and really mean it.

The thanksgiving psalms in the Bible celebrate the benefactions of God on behalf of the speaker. The Hebrew verb for "give thanks" (*yadah*) can also mean "profess, recount, commemorate, or praise." The word evokes the image of someone standing up in an assembly and pointing out for all to hear what God has done for the speaker. Some people describe it as "giving testimony." Many of the thanksgiving psalms seem to have been composed to accompany a thanksgiving sacrifice (*todah*) offered at the Jerusalem Temple. In these psalms the speaker recounts what God has done and invites others to join in praising the mercy and power of God. A thanksgiving psalm bears witness to a hope that has been fulfilled by God, and so provides further reason to rely on God as the ultimate reason for hope.

Psalm 30 is an individual thanksgiving. After expressing the intention to thank God ("I will extol you, O Lord"), the speaker provides a short description of the crisis (30:1-3), invites others to join in his thanks and praise to God (30:4-5), gives a longer and more detailed description of the crisis (30:6-10), and expresses his own feelings of joy as the recipient of God's help (30:11-12). While Psalm 30 contains many features that are characteristic of the biblical thanksgivings, it also presents us with some concepts that may seem strange or unfamiliar to us (though they are common enough in the Old Testament).

The psalmist first describes the crisis in 30:1-3 as a near death experience, and identifies God as the one responsible for his rescue. As in the laments, there is a strong sense of the existence of "foes" in whose presence he was being shamed because of his predicament. Also as in the laments, the crisis is described in vague terms, thus allowing others to identify with the psalmist's plight and to use the psalm to express their own sufferings. The terms "Sheol" and "Pit" refer to the abode of the dead. While the early parts of the Old Testament display some concept of life after death, it is hardly a place of eternal bliss or even conscious happiness (see below on 30:9). It is more like limbo than heaven, hell, or purgatory.

The invitation to God's "faithful ones" in 30:4-5 to join in the thanksgiving links the speaker's former sufferings to God's anger at him. But it also reminds them that God's favor is for a lifetime and that "joy comes with the morning."

The nature of the speaker's fault is hinted at in the longer description of his crisis in 30:6-10. There he admits that in his prosperity he arrogantly said, "I shall never be moved" and thought that he was a "strong mountain" favored by God (30:6-7). However, when God hid his face, then he found himself in dismay. Whether his suffering was physical or psychological is not clear. In either case the speaker felt that his life was at stake. He describes his petition in 30:8-10 as a challenge to God to act on his behalf and to recall (as if God needed reminding) that those who dwell in Sheol or the Pit cannot praise God. In other words, he suggests that if God wants more praise and honor from humans, it is in God's self-interest to rescue the psalmist from his "near death" crisis and let him live so that he may continue to praise God.

In his final comment (30:11-12) the psalmist uses two striking images: mourning turned into dancing, and replacing sackcloth with garments of joy. By way of conclusion he promises to give thanks to God forever. His thanksgiving psalm bears witness to a hope fulfilled by God (rescue from danger of death), and explains why in the future he can be a person of hope.

One of the terms used for the sacrament of ongoing Christian life is "Eucharist," based on a Greek word meaning thanksgiving. In the Eucharist many of the great themes and institutions of the Old Testament come together. The Eucharist is a commemoration of Passover, a memorial, a covenant meal, and a sign of hope for the coming kingdom of God. Some scholars have suggested that the Eucharist ought to be understood in terms of a thanksgiving sacrifice (*todah*). At the very least, this concept can help us to understand better the nature of the eucharistic prayers which recount what God has done on our behalf in and through Jesus Christ, with particular attention to Jesus' Last Supper with his friends as a sign of hope for the grand banquet to be celebrated in the kingdom of God. It also invites us all to join in giving thanks and praise to God always.

Questions: What do you understand by "thanksgiving"? How does your understanding compare with the biblical concept? Can saying "thank you" contribute to your capacity to be a more hopeful person?

11. REFUGE (PSALM 31)

"Be a rock of refuge for me, a strong fortress to save me." (Ps 31:2)

A refuge is a place of shelter or relief from danger. In many psalms the speaker prays for refuge. Several different terms are used to convey the same basic idea. An especially thick cluster of "refuge" images appears in Psalm 18:2: "The LORD is my rock, my fortress, and my deliverer, my God, my rock in whom I take refuge, my shield, and the horn of my salvation, my stronghold." These terms are spread throughout the book of Psalms and express what is perhaps the most fundamental hope expressed by the psalmists. They hope to find rest and security in God.

The idea that God is the only genuine refuge occurs throughout the Psalter. For example, Psalm 46 (which was the biblical basis for Martin Luther's famous hymn, "A Mighty Fortress Is Our God") begins by asserting that "God is our refuge and strength" and ends by affirming that "the God of Jacob is our refuge." For some other instances of the theme of God as refuge, see Psalms 14:6; 62:7-8; and 71:7. The psalmists hope for refuge and expect to find it only in God.

Psalm 31 is an individual lament, with the usual features found in that category of psalms: direct address to God (31:1), prayers of petition (31:1-4, 15-18), expressions of trust in God (31:5-8, 14), complaints (31:9-13), and a final word of deliverance or thanksgiving (31:19-24). Running through the entire psalm are expressions of hope to find refuge or shelter in God.

In the initial prayer of petition (31:1-4) the psalmist addresses God as Lord and affirms that "in you, O Lᴏʀᴅ, I seek refuge." He intersperses calls for help with acknowledgements of God as the "rock of refuge" and the "strong fortress." He pleads for God to deliver him from whatever crisis ("net") he is in, on the grounds that "you are my refuge."

In the first expression of trust in God (31:5-8), the psalmist commits himself to God ("Into your hand I commit my spirit") on the basis of his past experiences of God as redeemer. Having experienced God's steadfast love and having been delivered previously from "the hand of the enemy," he proclaims boldly, "I trust in the Lᴏʀᴅ" (31:6).

The complaint (31:9-13) describes the psalmist's sufferings on both the physical and the social-psychological levels. He claims that in his distress his "eye wastes away" from tears and that his "bones waste away." At the same time, he has become a social outcast, an object of scorn, shame, and dread to others. Nevertheless, his hope in God remains firm, so much so that in a second statement he affirms, "I trust in you, O Lᴏʀᴅ" (31:14). In another prayer of petition (31:15-18) he acknowledges his dependence on God ("My times are in your hand") and asks that God vindicate him and put his enemies to shame.

As in Psalm 22 and many other laments, the concluding section (31:19-24) suggests that the crisis is over and the psalmist is now giving thanks to God for his rescue. Here the language of refuge is prominent again. He begins by praising God's goodness toward those "who take refuge in you, in the sight of everyone" (31:19), and goes on in 31:20 to speak of God as providing "shelter" from human plots and slanders. The psalmist then compares life during his former crisis to being like "a city under siege" (31:21) and being driven far from God's presence (31:22). What God has provided for the psalmist is refuge and shelter.

By way of conclusion (31:23-24) the psalmist urges the "saints" to love the Lord. The saints are those who have been touched by God and so reflect the glory of the Holy One par excellence. The closing address to them to be strong and courageous characterizes the saints as "all you who wait for the Lord," an apt description of those who regard God as their refuge and hope in him.

According to Luke 23:46, one of Jesus' last words was based on Psalm 31:5: "Into your hands I commend my spirit." Throughout his gospel, Luke portrays Jesus as a model or exemplar for his readers. In his passion narrative Luke shows at several points that Jesus even in death remains faithful to and exemplifies perfectly his own teachings. One of Jesus' most prominent teachings was trust in God. Thus at the moment of his death on the cross, Jesus displays perfect trust in this heavenly Father by making his own the words of Psalm 31:5 and so incarnating the great themes of Psalm 31. In his Father he found refuge and shelter.

Questions: Do you look upon God as a refuge? From what do you hope to escape? How do you find safety and security in difficult times?

12. The Shadow of Your Wings (Psalm 36)

"How precious is your steadfast love, O God!
All people may take refuge in the shadow of your wings." (Ps 36:7)

The "shadow of your wings" is another image of refuge or shelter. The image of finding or taking refuge in "the shadow of your wings" appears not only in Psalm 36:7 but also in 57:1; 61:4; and 91:4. According to Psalm 17:8 one may "hide" there, and in 63:7 one can sing for joy there. While the basic meaning of refuge is clear enough, it may seem odd that ancient Israelites who rejected artistic depictions of their deity (see Exod 20:4) would talk as if their God had wings.

The image has a rich background. One of the familiar figures in ancient Near Eastern political and religious iconography was the cherub. These are large and imposing animal figures whose one common feature was their large wings. They functioned as symbolic representations of guardians, gatekeepers, and protectors. Two large cherubim made of olivewood were placed in the Holy of Holies in the Jerusalem Temple (see 1 Kgs 6:23-28). They were supposed to cover the ark of the covenant with their wings (see 1 Kgs 8:6-7; also Isa 6 and Ezek 10). Thus the cherubim served as the guardians of Yahweh's dwelling place on earth at the "mercy seat" above the ark of the covenant in the Jerusalem Temple. So finding refuge in "the shadow of his wings" meant being as close to the God of Israel as possible in the holiest part of the Jerusalem Temple, that is, where the winged cherubim were.

Psalm 36 is difficult to classify by literary form. On the basis of verses 7-8 it is categorized by some as a song of Zion. Others regard it as an individual lament, consisting of a complaint, a declaration of trust, and a prayer of petition. Still others view it as simply three short pieces joined together rather awkwardly.

The first part (36:1-4) is a description of the ways of the "wicked" such as we might find in a Jewish wisdom text (see Proverbs or Sirach). Whether the wicked are Gentiles or wayward Jews (or both) is not clear. The wicked are said to listen to the voice or "oracle" of transgression (rather than to the voice of wisdom or of God), and to be totally lacking in "fear of God," that is, the proper respect that is due to God as creator and sustainer of all. The wicked imagine that their evil deeds will never be discovered. Their words are deceitful and cannot be trusted; nothing that they do is wise or good. They lie around plotting mischief, walk in ways that are not good, and do not reject evil.

One might expect now a corresponding description of the wise and righteous, as in Psalm 1. Instead, Psalm 36:5-9 presents a short hymn about God's love for his people. In it two great biblical themes—covenant and temple—come together and provide a context for understanding the image of "the shadow of your wings."

A covenant is an agreement between two parties that gives formal structure to their relationship. The concept of covenant provided the ancient Israelites with a way of imagining their relationship with God. It became the framework for understanding what God had done for them and how they as God's people should respond. The Jerusalem Temple built by King Solomon in the early tenth century B.C.E. became the central shrine and focus of Israel's religious practice.

The attributes of God listed in Psalm 36:5-6 have their context in the covenant. God's steadfast love (*ḥesed* in Hebrew) and faithfulness describe the spirit in which God entered into the covenant relationship with Israel. God's righteousness (or justice) and judgments allude to the obligations and responsibilities incumbent upon them as God's people.

The references to the Jerusalem Temple in 36:7-8 as the refuge for God's people and as God's "house" are linked with the covenant through the image of "the shadow of your wings." The image evokes God's special presence in the Temple at the ark of the covenant where the winged cherubim are. Thus the two great biblical symbols of God's covenant love (*ḥesed*) and God's presence come together in this image of hope. The hymnic section ends in 36:9 by praising God for the gift of life with the images of the fountain and the light by which we see.

The psalm ends in 36:10-12 with a prayer of petition. The psalmist first asks God to continue his steadfast love and saving power to the wise and righteous. Then he begs for protection against the wicked persons described in 36:1-4.

Jesus seems to have respected the Jerusalem Temple as the center of Jewish religious practice, though in his own preaching and activity he subordinated it to the theme of the kingdom of God. In Luke 2:49 he speaks of it as his Father's house. However, he also appears to have been a critic of the practical operation of the Temple in his symbolic act of "cleansing" the Temple (Mark 11:15-19) and in his prophecy of its imminent destruction (Mark 13:2). These were undoubtedly factors in Jesus' condemnation and execution under Pontius Pilate (see Mark 14:58; 15:29). In his lament over Jerusalem in Matthew 23:37-39 Jesus evokes a variation on the "shadows of your wings" image and applies it to himself rather than his Father when he says, "How often have I desired to gather your children together as a hen gathers her brood under her wings, and you were not willing!"

Questions: How would you fill out the picture of the image of "the shadow of your wings"? What characteristics of God does the image suggest?

13. THE LAND (PSALM 37)

"For the wicked shall be cut off,
but those who wait for the Lord shall inherit the land." (Ps 37:9)

In most parts of the world, both in antiquity and today, acquiring land is a wise and important move. My great-grandfather came from Ireland to the United States of America in the late 1800s, made a lot of money quickly in copper mining, and returned to Ireland where he bought a large plot of land. Owning land not only provides a place to live but also in agrarian societies a source of food and revenue for one's family. Landowners generally wish to hand on their property to their children and thus insure security and continuity for the generations to come. To be driven off the land through military force or bankruptcy often means the end of family stability and identity.

In addition to the material benefits that owning land can bring, it also provides a sense of identity, stability, and continuity with both the past and the future. In this framework the land is an image of hope. Attachment to the land is, of course, not unique to the ancient Israelites. Indeed, the persistence of the hope of owning land underlies much of the strife in Israel/ Palestine today, what we customarily call the "Holy Land."

In ancient Israel owning land was a goal for many people. There was, however, also a sense that the land of Israel in particular really belonged to Yahweh, the God of Israel, who says in Leviticus 25:23, "the land is mine; with me you are but aliens and tenants." Nevertheless, the ancient Israelites were strongly attached to their ancestral lands, as the chilling episode of Naboth and Ahab in 1 Kings 21 illustrates.

The most prominent and recurrent image of hope in Psalm 37 is the land; see verses 3, 9, 11, 22, 29, and 34. The psalmist intends to encourage good persons who are puzzled by the apparent success and prosperity of others who seem to be wicked. He repeatedly uses the image of inheriting the land as a symbol of hope for those good people who remain faithful to their principles and wait for God to vindicate them. The corresponding recurrent image applied to the wicked is that of being "cut off," most likely from their land, or the land of the living, or from God (see 37:9, 22, 28, 34, 38).

Psalm 37 is generally classified as a wisdom psalm. It is perhaps more accurately described as a collection of aphorisms or wisdom sayings. There is no obvious connection with any temple ritual. In form and content it is closer to Proverbs and Sirach than to most of the other psalms. At two points (37:25 and 35-36) the speaker recounts personal experiences in the first-person singular. Most of the psalm consists of short statements (maxims) that attempt to summarize general human experiences in order to shape human behavior in the future. The Hebrew text takes the form of an acrostic. That is, each short section begins with a successive letter in the Hebrew alphabet: *aleph* = verses 1-2, *beth* = verses 3-4, *gimel* = verses 5-6, and so on. This device, which is used in other psalms (most massively in Psalm 119), gives the impression of its content being comprehensive and complete.

The main concern in Psalm 37 is to defend the law of retribution in the face of appearances to the contrary. According to this principle, the wise and righteous are rewarded, while the foolish and wicked are punished according to their deeds. The principle of retribution is affirmed in many parts of the Old Testament and was a staple of the ancient Near Eastern wisdom schools, though it is vigorously challenged in the books of Job and Ecclesiastes. Without appealing to a divine judgment after death, Psalm 37 insists that in this life the righteous will be vindicated ("inherit the land") and the wicked will be "cut off."

While the acrostic pattern of Psalm 37 makes it difficult to discern an outline, it is possible to distinguish four sections in the text: the contrasting destinies of the wicked and the righteous (37:1-11), the attacks of the wicked overcome (37:12-20), the eventual success of the righteous (37:21-26), and instructions for the righteous (37:27-40).

While not denying the apparent success of the wicked, the psalmist insists that their prosperity is only temporary and encourages the righteous to wait patiently for God to act on their behalf. The promise that they will eventually "inherit the land" is the lead image of hope to which he appeals throughout the psalm. Whereas the wicked will fade away like grass (37:2) and vanish like smoke (37:20), the righteous are repeatedly promised that they will "inherit the land."

Speaking in the first-person singular, the psalmist claims that in all his life "I have not seen the righteous forsaken or their children begging bread" (37:25). Would that this claim were true! Before rejecting his words too quickly, however, modern readers need to recognize that the sayings of the ancient sages were aiming at general (not total) validity, and that here the psalmist was trying to provide rhetorical encouragement and hope to dispirited persons rather than to formulate universally valid scientific laws.

It is generally recognized that the beatitude in Matt 5:5 ("Blessed are the meek, for they will inherit the earth") reflects the language of Psalm 37:11 ("But the meek shall inherit the land, and delight themselves in abundant prosperity"). The Matthean beatitude expands the scope of the promise and puts its fulfillment off to the full coming of God's kingdom. The hope that Jesus offers is not confined to the Holy Land or to the present life before death. With the development of the concepts of the kingdom of God, life after death, resurrection, and final divine judgment in Judaism and early Christianity, many of the apparently "foolish" assertions of Psalm 37 take on new meaning and validity.

Questions: Why is the land such a strong image of hope? Why do bad things happen to good people? Why do good things happen to bad people?

14. THE ROYAL WEDDING (PSALM 45)

"Therefore God, your God, has anointed you with the
oil of gladness beyond your companions." (Ps 45:7)

It may seem strange to find a royal wedding song in the book of Psalms. But the palace of the kings of Judah was close to the Jerusalem Temple, and so the celebration of a royal wedding became a religious event. There was also a political dimension associated with royal weddings in the ancient Near East. It was customary for royal families from different kingdoms to inter-marry as a means of forming and securing alliances. The practice is sometimes even described as "marrying one's enemies." So royal weddings in ancient Israel were hope-filled political events celebrated in a religious context.

In antiquity as in many parts of our world today, marriages between members of high-status families were arranged by the patriarchs of the respective families. There were often economic negotiations and legal documents giving structure to the new relationship. The bride and groom themselves may never have even met. Or if they did, their encounter would have been closely supervised by their elders. The last step in the process involved bringing the bride into the household of the groom. A very im-portant goal in a royal wedding was to produce male descen-dants who might eventually become kings and princes, and female descendants who might be part of other marriage alli-ances in the future.

Psalm 45 reflects the final stage in the wedding arrange-ments: the introduction of a non-Israelite princess into the royal household of Judah. This royal wedding song seems to have been composed for such an occasion and perhaps even sung as part of the ceremony at the palace. The progress of thought is somewhat hard to follow, since there appear to be several different speakers as well as changes of scene. However, a close reading of Psalm 45 can help us to sense the hopes that a royal wedding raised not only for the royal household but also for the people the king ruled.

The superscription labels Psalm 45 "a love song," and the psalmist in verse 1 describes his own hope to compose a poem worthy of such a great occasion. Then in verses 2-9a he describes the king in terms of his person (45:2), his role as king (45:3-7a), and his readiness for the wedding (45:7b-9). The king is praised as handsome, gracious, and blessed by God. It was the king's task to protect and defend his people by military and political means. And so the psalmist mentions his sword, steed, and arrows that are to be used "for the cause of truth and to defend the right" (45:4). The direct address "O God" in verse 6 is peculiar, since one might expect the king himself to be addressed at that point. Perhaps "God" was substituted for "king" when Israel's monarchy had ceased. Or maybe the address to God was meant to emphasize the divine support bestowed on the king. At any rate, the ideal king was to be the champion of equity and righteousness, and the enemy of the wicked.

According to Psalm 45:7b-9 the king and his retinue are ready to greet the bride. The king and his garments are fragrant with oil and spices, and pleasant music is being played on stringed instruments. He is accompanied by princesses and his own mother, "the queen." The queen mother, that is, the mother of the king, was the most prominent woman in ancient royal courts, especially when the king had more than one wife. In Psalm 45:10-12 the queen mother delivers her advice to the new bride. She tells the bride to forget her own people and her father's household, and to devote herself entirely to her new husband, the king. She should recognize what a good "catch" her son is and be satisfied with him.

In verses 13-15 the scene shifts to the wedding procession with the bride and her retinue as they enter the king's house. The bride's splendor and the joy accompanying her entrance are emphasized. Just as the king was blessed in verses 3-6, so the new queen is blessed in verses 16-17. The hope is that she will produce sons who can succeed their father, and so she will be praised forever.

The royal wedding song in Psalm 45 reflects the hopes that ancient Israel associated with their kings and queens. In that context a royal wedding was a grand occasion and a reason for hope for the future. In Matthew 22:1-14 Jesus compares the kingdom of God to the wedding of a king's son. Just as one would not lightly refuse an invitation to such a great event and would appear in proper attire, so his hearers should respond to Jesus' invitation to the kingdom of God and act in appropriate ways. Likewise with the parable of the bridesmaids awaiting the bridal party's approach to the groom's household in Matthew 25:1-13, Jesus encourages an attitude of constant preparedness and watchfulness in the face of the coming kingdom of God. These two parables give a glimpse of the hopes surrounding a royal wedding in antiquity and how they were transformed by Jesus to teach about the kingdom of God.

Questions: Why are weddings a sign of hope? What special significance do royal weddings have? In what sense is a royal wedding an image of hope for the kingdom of God?

15. THE KINGDOM OF GOD (PSALM 47)

> *"God has gone up with a shout,*
> *the LORD with the sound of a trumpet."* (Ps 47:5)

Ancient Israel was a little people with a big idea. They occupied a small strip of land on the eastern Mediterranean coast between the Egyptians to the south and the Syrians, Assyrians, Babylonians, and Persians to the north and east. Thus they often found themselves to be the battleground between more powerful neighbors. When the various tribes organized themselves into a confederacy and then chose a king around 1000 B.C.E., they enjoyed glimmers of power and prominence under David and Solomon. But they soon fell back generally to being the doormat of ancient Near Eastern politics.

However, this little people never lost hope because they had a big idea: the kingdom of God. They believed that Yahweh was not only their national God but also the greatest God of all. They believed that Yahweh was the creator and sustainer of the universe, and that he had chosen them to be his special people. There were historical tensions between their claims for the divine king and the pretensions of their human kings. But on the ideal level they attributed whatever good their human kings achieved to the divine king. And they believed that Yahweh reigned not only over their land but also over all the earth and even over the heavens above. This big idea of the kingdom of God is why the Hebrew Bible is preeminently a book of hope.

It appears that the people of ancient Israel celebrated liturgically the kingship of Yahweh in the fall of each year with a great festival at the Jerusalem Temple. Psalm 47 may well have been composed for that occasion. (See also Psalms 24, 29, 93, and 96–99 for other psalms with possible links to that festival.) The fact that Psalm 47 now appears between two songs of Zion (46 and 48) adds to its possible connection to a celebration at the Jerusalem Temple. Reading Psalm 47 in that context can help us to understand better what the ancient Israelites believed about their God and why they continued to be a people of hope.

Psalm 47 is classified as a psalm about the kingship of God and seems to reflect a liturgical celebration of that theme. It contains an invitation to all nations to join the celebration (47:1-4), a glimpse of the ceremony itself (47:5-7), and a closing proclamation of God's reign (47:8-9).

The invitation (47:1-4) identifies the Lord (Yahweh) in grandiose terms as the "Most High" and as the "Great King" over all the earth. It praises his victories over other peoples (perhaps alluding to the exploits of David and Solomon) and his choice of Israel as the people whom he loves in a special way. The invitation urges "all you peoples" to join in clapping and singing for the greatness of this God.

The central section (47:5-7) states that "God has gone up with a shout." What does it mean to say that God "has gone up"? Some scholars think that it refers to a temple ritual in which the ark of the covenant was paraded around in a procession and eventually returned to its place in the Holy of Holies. In this ritual the ark symbolized the presence of Yahweh as king and its placement in the Holy of Holies was a kind of ritual enthronement (see Ps 132:7-9). This ritual enthronement was accompanied by shouting, trumpet blasts, and lots of singing (the verb "sing" appears five times in vv. 6-7). The message of the whole celebration was that "God is king of all the earth" (Ps 47:7).

The final proclamation (47:8-9) insists that God reigns over the nations (on earth) and sits on his holy throne (in heaven). The kingdom of God is not a place (like England, France, or Spain). Rather it is more a dynamic entity, that is, a reigning— more a verb than a noun. The psalm closes by reaffirming God's sovereignty over the "princes of the peoples," symbolized by his possessing their "shields." In other words, he has disarmed them. The final phrase ("he is highly exalted") returns to the theme of the enthronement of Yahweh as supreme in heaven and on earth.

Not long after the institution of human kingship ended in ancient Israel, the big idea of the kingdom of God took on new life. There was a shift in perspective from the past and present to the future. Instead of emphasizing the past and present dimensions of God's reign, some Jews looked forward to the future, definitive display of the kingdom of God. This hope, of course, became the central theme in Jesus' teaching and activity (see Mark 1:14-15). And he taught us all to pray, "Thy kingdom come!" (Matt 6:10).

Questions: How might an annual celebration of God's kingship have increased hope among the ancient Israelites? What do you mean when you pray, "Thy kingdom come"? Is God's kingdom primarily a present or future reality for you?

16. THE CITY OF GOD (PSALM 48)

> *"Great is the LORD and greatly to be*
> *praised in the city of our God."* (Ps 48:1)

Jerusalem today is not a museum. As part of my graduate biblical studies I spent a year in Jerusalem. Almost every afternoon I took a walk around the Old City. People live and work there, and bring their own sufferings, joys, and hopes along with them. The most famous part of Jerusalem is the Temple Mount, once the site of the Jerusalem Temple and now the place of the Muslim shrine known as the Dome of the Rock and the Al-Aqsa Mosque. The ancient name of the Temple Mount was Mount Zion. It remains a place of great symbolic significance and political controversy.

As seen in our discussion of Psalm 15, mountains are images of hope. On mountains many of us somehow feel closer to God. For the ancient Israelites, Mount Zion with its Temple and royal palace became a major vehicle for both the primal religious yearnings of God's people and the mythology that pervaded the ancient Near East. As the song of Zion known as Psalm 48 illustrates, Mount Zion was a symbol of Yahweh's power and covenant love. (For other Songs of Zion, see Psalms 46, 76, 84, 87, and 122.) In reading these psalms it is important to keep in mind that they celebrate the presence of God among us and are not travel commercials aimed at prospective tourists.

As a Song of Zion, Psalm 48 begins (48:1-3) and ends (48:12-14) with descriptions of the grandeur of ancient Jerusalem as the place of God's presence par excellence. Between those two sections there are descriptions of a failed attack on the city of God (48:4-8) and a celebration of God's power and covenant love in thwarting that attack (48:9-11).

The opening section (48:1-3) is a call to praise Yahweh especially with regard to his presence at Mount Zion, that is, at the Jerusalem Temple. The importance and grandeur of that place are described with seven striking phrases: "city of our God," "holy mountain," "beautiful in elevation," "joy of all the earth," "in the far north," "city of the great King," and "sure defense." All these epithets emphasize the city of God as holy and secure, set apart from ordinary life, and a refuge for those in need. Its description as "joy of all the earth" takes the Temple beyond the confines of the Holy Land and gives it a universal significance. The most puzzling epithet is "in the far north." Jerusalem, of course, is in the southern part of the Holy Land. The allusion here seems to be to Mount Zaphon, on the border between Turkey and Syria today, which was once regarded as the home of the Canaanite storm-god, Baal. Here the epithet "in the far north" has been transferred to Israel's God, Yahweh, thus expanding the range of his sovereignty.

The description of the attack by hostile kings in verses 4-8 may refer to an actual failed military siege of Jerusalem. Or it may have mythological roots in the narrative of Yahweh's over-coming the powers of chaos and imposing order and stability on the world (see Gen 1). In either interpretation, the point is that when Yahweh's foes saw this splendid and secure city, they were amazed and frightened. Their reactions are compared first to the trembling that overcomes a woman in labor with a child and then to ships battered by strong winds at sea. The hostile kings recognize Jerusalem as the city of the Lord of hosts, that is, the city of the all-powerful God who rules over all creation and who can summon all the forces of creation to carry out his purposes.

The celebration of Yahweh's effortless victory (48:9-11) links Mount Zion and its Temple with God's steadfast (or, covenantal) love for his people. Here, however, the focus shifts from Yah-weh's display of power to his just governance of the universe. What is stressed here is Yahweh's "justice" (not "victory" as in the NRSV) and "judgments" (or decrees). These have signifi-cance not only for Jerusalem and environs ("its daughters") but also for "the ends of the earth."

This song of Zion closes in verses 12-14 with an invitation to walk around the holy city and to admire its grandeur. The reason for the tour is to enable one to tell "the next generation" that in this city God has made a dwelling place on earth and promised to guide his people forever.

Jerusalem as the city of God, with its Temple and royal palace, was a symbol of hope for ancient Israel from the time of Solomon in the early tenth century B.C.E. to its first destruction in 587 B.C.E. The complex was rebuilt after the return from exile, greatly expanded under Herod the Great, and destroyed again by the Romans in 70 C.E. Nevertheless, the city of God did not cease to be an image of hope for God's people. The prophecies of Ezekiel and Second Isaiah (see Isa 40–55) have nurtured the religious imaginations of Jews and Christians for many centuries. Many of Jesus' contemporaries spent much time and energy either in beautifying the Temple as part of Herod's ambitious building program or in drawing up plans for a still more perfect city of God (see the *Temple Scroll* and the New Jerusalem texts among the Dead Sea scrolls).

The final pages of the Christian Bible (see Rev 21:1–22:5) describe the "New Jerusalem" descending from heaven to earth. That city will have no external lighting and no temple because God's presence with Christ the Lamb will supply all that is needed with regard to God's power and covenant love. The hopes associated with the city of God will be fulfilled with the full coming of God's kingdom.

Questions: Are there specific places where you have felt especially close to God? How do you react to statements about Zion as God's dwelling place on earth? How do you assess hopes for the New Jerusalem?

17. A CLEAN HEART (PSALM 51)

"Create in me a clean heart, O God,
and put a new and right spirit within me." (Ps 51:10)

One of the most elemental hopes for humans is forgiveness. In our social relationships when we recognize that we have offended someone (especially someone whom we respect and/or love), we feel the need to apologize and to make amends in some way. Likewise, in our relationship with God, when we sin, we try to repair the relationship by confessing our sin, asking for forgiveness, and promising to do better. In ancient Israel such efforts were often accompanied by the sacrifice of an animal or some other material goods. From these actions we hope to obtain forgiveness and reconciliation either from another person or (especially) from God.

Psalm 51:10 asks God for a "clean heart" and a "right spirit." In the biblical understanding of the human person, the "heart" is not so much the place of emotion or romance as it is the center of the person, including the intelligence and will. To ask God for a "clean heart" means to seek for a fresh start as a person. Likewise in biblical anthropology, the "spirit" is the life-energy that God puts into the human person, the breath of life by which we live (see Gen 2:7). To pray for a "new and right spirit" is to call for a renewed and steadfast relationship with God. These hopes can only be fulfilled when one recognizes and confesses one's sin, throws oneself on God's mercy, and resolves to amend one's life and to move in new and positive directions.

Psalm 51 is usually classified as an individual lament. It addresses God directly, laments the present situation, professes trust in God, asks for rescue, and ends with a reference to sacrifice. However, unlike most laments where the suffering is due to external forces or circumstances, here the speaker acknowledges personal responsibility for the anguish and guilt being experienced. In Christian tradition, Psalm 51 has been classified as one of the seven penitential psalms along with Psalms 6, 32, 38, 102, 139, and 143.

The superscription to Psalm 51 associates it with David's adultery with Bathsheba and his heinous crime in arranging for her husband, Uriah the Hittite, to be killed in battle (see 2 Sam 11–12). While the generic language of Psalm 51 is not exhausted by those incidents, its application to David's sin is certainly appropriate.

Psalm 51 consists of two main sections (51:1-9, 10-17), plus what might be called an appendix or a later "correction." The first main section contains a plea for divine mercy (51:1-2), a confession of sin (51:3-6), and a further plea for divine mercy (51:7-9). The image of blotting out sins appears at the beginning (51:1) and end (51:9), and in between there is much talk about washing and cleansing. In verses 3-6 the psalmist admits to having sinned against God and agrees that his sins deserve punishment. But his appeal is to God's mercy in the hope that divine mercy will override divine justice. When the psalmist says that he was born guilty and was a sinner from the moment of conception, the idea is that he has always been a sinner before God. Psalm 51:5 is better understood as rhetorical exaggeration (hyperbole) than as a condemnation of sexual relations or as biblical proof for the doctrine of original sin.

The second major section (51:10-17) begins (51:10) and ends (51:17) with references to "heart" and "spirit." It consists of further pleas for forgiveness from and reconciliation with God (51:10-12), promises to teach others the ways of God and to praise God (51:13-15), and reflections about the superiority of spiritual sacrifices over material sacrifices (51:16-17). The usual way to be reconciled with God was to offer material sacrifices at the Temple (a holocaust or sin-offering). Psalm 51, however, asserts that the sacrifice most acceptable to God is "a broken spirit, a broken and contrite heart" (51:17). The "correction" in verses 18-19 suggests that once the Jerusalem Temple is rebuilt, material sacrifices will again be acceptable and pleasing to God.

The application of Psalm 51 to David reminds us that forgiveness of sin is always possible with God. The sins that David committed—adultery and murder—were terrible. Nevertheless, David's hope for forgiveness became a reality through his contrition and reliance on God's mercy. As a result, God created in David "a clean heart" and "a new and right spirit."

As the Son of David, Jesus proclaimed the need for repentance and conversion in the face of the coming kingdom of God (see Mark 1:15). His parable in Luke 18:9-14 holds up as a model of genuine prayer the words of the tax collector: "God, be merciful to me, a sinner." And his parables of the lost (sheep, coin, and son) in Luke 15 show how eagerly God wishes to show mercy to repentant sinners.

Questions: Has any experience of forgiveness and reconciliation in your life been a source of new hope for you? Was the forgiveness from another person? Was it from God? Or were you the one to offer forgiveness?

18. THE OLIVE TREE (PSALM 52)

> *"But I am like a green olive tree in the house of God.*
> *I trust in the steadfast love of God forever and ever."* (Ps 52:8)

Olive trees are a common sight in the Holy Land and other Mediterranean countries. They grow slowly but reach heights of between twenty and forty feet. They are solid and sturdy, and can produce fruit for hundreds of years. In Psalm 52:8 the green olive tree serves as a symbol of trust and hope in God.

In biblical times (as today), one of the most disturbing experiences for good and righteous persons was to see scoundrels and evildoers prosper and even boast about their success. Such a sight is not only galling on the personal level but also raises questions about the justice of God. How could God allow wicked persons to prosper while righteous ones suffer? Questions about God's justice come up in every age and are prominent in both the Old and New Testament.

Psalm 52 explores a situation in which the wicked seem to be prospering and the righteous seem to be suffering. Although it has some features of an individual lament, it is probably better described as a psalm of trust. It consists of a denunciation of the prosperous scoundrel (52:1-4), a warning about the impending divine judgment upon him (52:5-7), and the psalmist's own expression of trust and hope in God (52:8-9).

The scoundrel denounced in verses 1-4 is addressed in a mocking way as "O mighty one." The Hebrew word *gibbor* can also be translated as "hero." This hero is described as spending his energies in boasting over and plotting mischief against the righteous. His weapons are not the sword and shield of the warrior but rather his tongue, which is compared to a sharp razor. He is said to enjoy lying words more than speaking the truth. His words are devouring and deceitful. The bitter and harsh tone of the description is clearly not an example of love of enemies or turning the other cheek.

The warning about the coming divine judgment on the scoundrel in verse 5 uses four very strong words to describe what God is going to do to him: break down, snatch, tear, and uproot. The image of uprooting is especially effective in preparing for the image of the green olive tree in verse 8. It is not easy to uproot a large and sturdy olive tree. In verses 6-7 the scene shifts from the punishment of the wicked to the vindication of the righteous. When they view the downfall of the wicked, the righteous will both fear (it could happen to them if they ever take the way of the wicked) and laugh (continuing the mockery implied in the initial address to the "mighty one"). What is at stake here is the eternal human question: In what or in whom do you trust? According to verse 7, the scoundrel puts his trust in his riches rather than in God. The familiar image of God as the only genuine "refuge" provides the bridge to the psalmist's own affirmation of trust and hope in God.

In verses 8-9 the psalmist compares himself to a "green olive tree." The image conveys connotations of strength and sturdiness, great size and many years of life, and fruitfulness. The "house of God" is sometimes taken as an allusion to a place in the Jerusalem Temple compound, some kind of garden set apart for shade perhaps. The three verbs used by the psalmist to describe his response to God—trust, thank, and proclaim (or, wait for)—make the point that his trust and hope are in God, not in himself or in his possessions. He interprets the impending downfall of the scoundrel as an act of divine justice and retribution. In response to what God is about to do (which is as good as his having already done it), he promises to trust in God's steadfast love, to thank God forever, and to proclaim God's name.

The German word *Schadenfreude* refers to taking delight in the misfortunes of an enemy. To some extent Psalm 52 is an example of this very human emotion. Even the best of us occasionally enjoy seeing villains get the just punishments that we think they deserve. If nothing else, it reminds us that sometimes there is justice even in this life. Of course, in Psalm 52 it is God, not the psalmist, who administers justice. This psalm also reminds us of Jesus' pronouncement "you cannot serve God and wealth" (Matt 6:24) and the challenge involved in his admonition to break the cycle of human vengeance by trying to love one's enemies (Matt 5:44).

Questions: Does the success of scoundrels dampen your hope? Who do you expect to administer justice? When and where?

19. THE ROCK (PSALM 62)

> *"He alone is my rock and my salvation, my fortress;*
> *I shall never be shaken."* (Ps 62:2)

One of the common images for God in the Psalms is that of the rock. The contexts assume that this is a very large rock, solid and sturdy and not easily moved. In Psalm 62 and elsewhere the rock appears alongside images of God as refuge and as fortress. This rock provides safety and security. On it one can put aside one's fears and anxieties and find rest. The rock is an image of hope in that with God it may be possible to enjoy peace and calm even in the midst of a chaotic world.

Psalm 62 is a psalm of trust. In it the psalmist speaks for himself (62:1-2), addresses his enemies (62:3-4), speaks again for himself (62:5-7), addresses the community (62:8-10), and speaks once more for himself (62:11-12). There are also alternations between direct discourse and third-person description. These shifts contribute to the message of the psalm that arriving at perfect trust and hope in God is something of a struggle.

In verses 1-2 the psalmist describes his own state of soul. He is waiting silently and confidently for God to act on his behalf. He hopes that God will take the initiative precisely because he trusts in God as his rock and fortress. The word "alone" appears in each of his statements about God's care for him. The term "salvation" in this context probably does not carry all the rich spiritual connotations attached to it in the New Testament and Christian theology. Rather, it refers more concretely to the rescue and healing in the context of earthly existence here and now. The psalmist claims to share the solidity that pertains to God as his rock. Therefore he can claim, "I shall never be shaken."

The psalmist's comment about his enemies consists of a direct rebuke of them (62:3) and a description of their behavior (62:4). He contends that these enemies are battering him (or some other victim) as if he were "a leaning wall, a tottering fence." He accuses them of seeking to bring down prominent persons (including the psalmist?) by lies and deception.

In his second statement about himself (62:5-7) the psalmist uses the same terms as in verses 1-2. Again he stresses that God "alone" is his rock, salvation, and fortress. Again he describes his own stance as silent and confident waiting, and professes that he will not be shaken. He adds that God is the source of his deliverance and honor, and describes God further as "my mighty rock, my refuge" (62:7). The repetition and expansion of verses 1-2 here suggest that the psalmist is trying to deepen his trust and hope in God by further assimilating the images of rock, refuge, and fortress.

In addressing the wider community ("O people") in verses 8-10 the psalmist exhorts them to share his vision and experience of God ("God is a refuge for us") and to recognize that in God's eyes noble and wealthy persons are of no more account than the poor and lowly. When weighed in the scales used by God, neither group makes much of an impression. The moral message drawn from the image of the scales is that money and other possessions will not bring about the security and peace to be found in God as the rock, fortress, and refuge par excellence.

In the final stanza (62:11-12) the psalmist describes an oracle that he has heard from God concerning God's power, steadfast love, and justice. These three attributes are basic to God's covenant relationship with Israel as his people. This special relationship is the foundation of Israel's trust and hope in God throughout the Old Testament.

Psalm 62 is noteworthy for its several images of God that inspire hope. At the same time it suggests that it is not enough merely to say the right words, or to imagine that hope is something that one can obtain once and for all time. Rather, hope must grow and deepen in the context of the struggles of everyday life, prayer, and good works. When at the end of the Sermon on the Mount Jesus urges his followers to build their houses on rock (Matt 7:24), he picks up the biblical image of God as the rock and uses it to describe his own wise teachings and his status as the Son of God.

Questions: When God is described as a "rock," what image comes to your mind? What characteristics of God does the image convey to you? Is hope ever a struggle for you?

20. RAIN (PSALM 65)

> *"You visit the earth and water it, you greatly enrich it;*
> *the river of God is full of water;*
> *you provide the people with grain,*
> *for so you have prepared it."* (Ps 65:9)

The climate in the Holy Land is quite regular (but not absolutely so). There is a rainy season from October to April, and the rest of the year is dry. Water is very important to the people who live there. In Jesus' time farming was a major occupation, and the calendar to a large extent revolved around the agricultural cycle. If the rain failed to materialize in any year, the result might be unemployment for many and even famine. The people hoped for the rain to come in such a way as to yield a bountiful harvest.

Psalm 65 is communal thanksgiving. Its three parts concern gathering in the Jerusalem Temple (65:1-4), praising God as the Creator and Lord of all the earth (65:5-8), and thanking God for the rain and the abundant harvest produced by it (65:9-13). What brings these three parts together into some kind of literary unity seems to be the celebration of the Jewish festival of Tabernacles (also known as *Sukkot* in Hebrew and "Booths" in English).

The festival takes its name from the make-shift tents that ancient Israelite agricultural workers erected in the fields during harvest time so as not to waste time and energy traveling to and from the fields. Along with Passover and Weeks (or Pentecost), Tabernacles became a pilgrimage festival lasting eight days in which Jews were expected to go to Jerusalem and offer thanks-giving sacrifices in the Temple (see Deut 16:13-17). Tabernacles took place in the early fall (late September–early October), that is, at the end of the harvest and at the beginning of the rainy season. As one agricultural cycle was ending, a new one was starting.

The description of the gathering at the Jerusalem Temple (65:1-4) suggests that the people there were offering sacrifices in fulfillment of vows made to God during the growing season. They apparently promised that if God would grant them an abundant harvest, they would come to the Temple to praise God and offer material sacrifices in thanksgiving. They were there because their prayers had been answered. Their sins had not prevented the rain from coming, since God had forgiven them. The use of the Hebrew verb *kipper* in verse 3 may allude to the recently celebrated Yom Kippur (the Day of Atonement), when the people's sins had been "wiped away." The gathering at the Temple "in Zion" reflects the status of Tabernacles as a pilgrim-age feast when special sacrifices were to be offered at the Temple.

The central section (65:5-8) celebrates God's sovereignty over all creation. Addressing the "God of our salvation," the psalmist proclaims God to be "the hope of all the ends of the earth" (65:5). With the rain and the subsequent harvest, God had rescued his people from possible starvation and therefore can be praised as the ground or reason for the people's trust and hope for the future. Hope fulfilled begets more hope. In imposing order on the chaos at Creation (see Gen 1), God had proved his power over the seas and showed that now he can and does use the waters for salutary and constructive purposes. Too much rain (a flood) is as bad as too little.

The third section (65:9-13) focuses on God's provident use of rain to bring about a bountiful harvest. The description of God bringing the rains is told in loving detail in verses 9-10. The imagery there captures the divine guidance supplying just the right amount of rain to produce the harvest. In this way God is said to "crown the year with your bounty" (65:11). In verses 12-13 the psalmist uses several clothing metaphors—the hills girded with joy, the meadows clothed with flocks, and the valleys decked with grain—to describe the richness and beauty of the harvest. Just as Psalm 65 began with a word of praise ("Praise is due to you, O God"), so it closes with the image of the fields shouting and singing for joy.

According to John 7, Jesus went to Jerusalem to celebrate the feast of Tabernacles. There he entered the Temple compound and began to teach. On the last day of the festival he offered an invitation that was very appropriate to that festival and very much in the spirit of Psalm 65: "Let anyone who is thirsty come to me, and let anyone who believes in me drink" (John 7:37-38).

Questions: Why is rain an image of hope? Why is the harvest an image of hope? What do these images say about God?

21. THE EXODUS (PSALM 66)

> *"He turned the sea into dry land;*
> *they passed through the river on foot.*
> *There we rejoiced in him."* (Ps 66:6)

Ancient Israel's exodus from Egypt under Moses' leadership (see Exod 14–15) and their entrance into the land of Canaan under Joshua (see Josh 3) were among the most pivotal events in the formation of Israel as the people of God. The ancient Israelites interpreted these events (and everything in between them) as manifestations of the sovereignty of Yahweh, the God of Israel. Jews and Christians alike have taken these events not only as God's mighty acts in the past but also as the ground or reason for hope throughout the centuries and for the future.

The phrase "there we rejoiced in him" in Psalm 66:6 suggests that these events belong not only to the distant past but also to the present and we can now participate in them. We are somehow there. People today share in the exodus event by celebrating the Jewish Passover rituals and the Christian Eucharist. From a liturgical-theological perspective, the Exodus is an event of the past, present, and future.

Psalm 66 is a thanksgiving psalm. After an initial call to praise God (66:1-4), there is a communal thanksgiving (66:5-12) that appeals to the Exodus and to God's (more recent?) rescue of his people. Then there is an individual thanksgiving (66:13-20) consisting of a promise to offer material sacrifices at the Temple and a narration of what God has done.

There are two interpretive problems in Psalm 66. Who is the speaker and what rescue is being celebrated? There is a shift between the second and third sections from "we" language to "I" language. Some speculate that the speaker is the king who first uses the imperial "we" and then performs ("I") the thanksgiving sacrifice on behalf of the people. The rescue may be the Exodus throughout. Or it may have been that a more recent national rescue was interpreted in light of the exodus event. Most scholars today take it to be a separate and more recent event.

The call to praise God in verses 1-4 is directed to "all the earth," which is invited twice to sing praises to the God of Israel. The objects of the praises are the mighty acts of God, the foremost of these being Israel's miraculous escape from slavery in Egypt under Moses.

The communal thanksgiving ("we") in verses 5-12 begins by inviting all the earth to "see what God has done." His turning the sea into dry land alludes to ancient Israel's crossing the Reed

Sea, and the passing through the river refers to Joshua crossing the Jordan to enter the Promised Land. The combination follows the dynamic of the Song of Moses in Exodus 15 where the Exodus (15:4-10) leads to the entrance into the land (15:16-17), and both events issue in an affirmation of Yahweh's absolute sovereignty: "The Lord will reign forever and ever" (15:18).

With the Exodus providing the pattern or paradigm for God's mighty acts, the people of earth are invited in verses 8-12 to contemplate what seems to have been a more recent example of Yahweh's saving power on his people's behalf. Whatever the event was, it is attributed to God's saving power and is described with various images—forging silver in the fire, being caught in a net, bearing burdens on the back, and so on—as a kind of test by which through God's favor Israel was able to reach "a spacious place," that is, a place of security and safety.

The individual thanksgiving ("I") in verses 13-20 provides precious information about thanksgiving sacrifices offered in the Jerusalem Temple. In verses 13-15 the psalmist promises to offer various animals—rams, bulls, and goats—as holocausts (burnt offerings) to fulfill his vows. He seems to have vowed to offer such sacrifices if God would rescue him (or his people) from the danger. An integral part of the thanksgiving sacrifice was telling the story of the rescue (66:16-20). The psalmist insists that the rescue took place in response to his prayers to God, and points to God as the primary figure in the rescue. The narration ends with a blessing of God for having heard his prayer (66:20).

In Psalm 66 the Exodus from Egypt provides the paradigm for God's mighty acts and so a good reason for trusting and hoping in God at other points in Jewish (and Christian) history. For example, when the prophet known as Second Isaiah (see Isa 40–55) sought to convince Jewish exiles in Babylon to return to Jerusalem, he appealed especially to the Exodus as the basis for hoping that there could ever be a renewal of God's people in Jerusalem. Likewise, the fact that Jesus' death and resurrection took place at Passover (the celebration of the Exodus) led early

Christians to regard the Exodus as a type or foreshadowing of the paschal mystery.

Questions: Why did the Exodus of ancient Israel from Egypt play such a prominent role in the Psalms? What does it have to do with hope for the future? How do Jews and Christians participate in this event today?

22. THE IDEAL KING (PSALM 72)

> *"Give the king your justice, O God,*
> *and your righteousness to a king's son."* (Ps 72:1)

In ancient Israel the king was an important image of hope, as we have seen already from the psalms about the king's anointing and coronation (Ps 2) and about the royal wedding (Ps 45). The king was expected to be the enforcer of justice (judge), governor of his people (ruler), and symbol of strength and prestige among the other nations (warrior).

Psalm 72 is a royal psalm. The superscription associates it with Solomon. That fits well with Solomon as David's son, famous for his wisdom and the recipient of gifts from Sheba (see 1 Kgs 10). The text of the psalm prays that the king may be an instrument of God's justice (72:1-4), that he may have a long life (72:5-7), that he may exercise sovereignty and be respected by other kings (72:8-11), that he may act as a protector of the poor (72:12-14), and that he and his people may be blessed by God (72:15-17). Though probably not originally part of Psalm 72, the doxology (72:18-19) fits well into it. Its main function, however, is to round off the second of the five "books" or collections that make up the canonical book of Psalms.

In verses 1-4 the psalmist asks God to endow the king with his own justice or righteousness so that he might govern his people according to it. The result will be prosperity for the people and the king. He is given a special charge to defend and care for the poor and to crush the oppressors. Thus he will enforce God's own preferential option for the poor.

The prayer for the king's long life in verses 5-7 evokes images of the sun and moon and their long (eternal) duration. It also uses similes about the king being like rain falling on mown grass and showers watering the earth to describe the two great effects that his good leadership can bring: justice and peace.

The king is to be Israel's representative among the nations. In verses 8-11 the psalmist expresses the hope that the king will have a wide dominion ("from sea to sea"—perhaps from the Mediterranean Sea to the Persian Gulf), that he will force his enemies into submission so that they "lick the dust," and that all the kings of the earth will offer him tribute and homage.

The special concern that Israel's king is to have for the needy is stressed again even more strongly in verses 12-14. He is to be the instrument by which God's care for the poor is carried out. The king is to rescue them from oppression and violence, and their condition is to be as precious in the king's sight as it is in God's sight.

The final prayer is for God's blessings on the king and his people. The blessings include his long life and good name among his own people and among the nations, as well as bountiful harvests and good fortune for the people. The doxology in verses 18-19 is a reminder that the success of the king and his people depends on God and reflects the glory of God.

Few if any kings (including Solomon) in ancient Israel's history lived up to the high hopes and standards expressed in Psalm 72. The books of Kings tell a dreary tale about the repeated failures of the kings of Israel and Judah from Solomon to the Exile in the sixth century B.C.E. Nevertheless, there always remained among the people the hope that God would raise up a new king who might embody the ideals expressed in Psalm 72 and related literature.

Christians believe that these hopes were fulfilled at least in part by Jesus of Nazareth, a son of David. He embodied God's justice and righteousness. He lives forever. All nations recognize and honor him. He took up the cause of the poor. And his name endures forever. The one key factor not covered in Psalm 72 is the mystery of the cross, that is, Jesus' suffering and death. Through the cross Jesus redefined kingship and deepened God's relationship with humankind, especially with the needy.

Questions: What did ancient Israelites expect from their kings? How was the king to be an instrument of God? How was the king to provide hope for the poor?

23. NEARNESS TO GOD (PSALM 73)

> *"But for me it is good to be near God;*
> *I have made the Lord God my refuge,*
> *to tell of all your works."* (Ps 73:28)

Why do good things seem to happen to bad people? In Psalm 73 we return to this theme (see entry for Psalm 52). The question is as real today as it was in biblical times. According to the law of retribution, which is prominent in many parts of the Bible, good and wise persons are to prosper while wicked and foolish persons are to suffer punishment. But things do not always work out that way. The problem deepens when we try to discern God's role in all this. How can an omnipotent and just God allow the wicked to prosper and the righteous to suffer? This is the problem of theodicy.

Psalm 73 is a wisdom psalm. The law of retribution was a basic principle of ancient Near Eastern wisdom writings. While generally accepted in the books of Proverbs and Sirach, it is questioned by Ecclesiastes and subjected to a full-scale critique in the book of Job. Psalm 73 is an honest exploration of the problem. While it does not solve it intellectually, it finds an experiential and religious solution in nearness to God. Being close to God is put forward as the highest good for humans, while absence or estrangement from God is the worst evil. In one of the most beautiful images in the entire Bible, the psalmist says to God, "I am continually with you; you hold my right hand" (73:23).

After describing his puzzlement at the prosperity of the wicked (73:1-3), the psalmist describes what he saw and what he heard regarding the wicked (73:4-12). Then he explains his anguish and his subsequent change of perspective (73:13-17), and how he came to view in a new way the "end" or outcome of the wicked and the righteous (73:18-27). The final verse (73:28) summarizes the psalmist's discovery about the importance of closeness to God.

Psalm 73 is not so much a song to be sung by a choir or community as it is an individual's meditation on a topic. The psalmist begins in verse 1 by restating the law of retribution: "Truly God is good to the upright, to those who are pure in heart." But then in verses 2-3 he expresses doubt and confusion over the prosperity of the wicked. This inconsistency caused him almost to lose his trust and hope in God.

The description of the wicked in verses 4-12 seems remarkably contemporary. The psalmist first in verses 4-7 recounts what he saw: The wicked look well and seem free of trouble, though both on the outside and inside they are full of folly and wickedness. Then in verses 8-12 he describes what he hears from the wicked and from the people who admire them. The wicked scoff at God and threaten their opponents. Many people in turn praise the wicked and exhibit a kind of practical atheism. They ask cynically (as many do today), "How can God know? Is there knowledge in the Most High?" (73:11).

In verses 13-17 the psalmist describes his anguish at the situation. Even though he had kept his own heart clean, his puzzlement at the prosperity of the wicked disturbed him greatly. He found no value in simply complaining about injustice and feared that it might only further discourage other righteous persons. The prospect of studying the problem in depth (as in the book of Job) seemed wearisome. But while at the Jerusalem Temple he experienced a flash of insight that he expresses here somewhat vaguely, "I perceived their end" (73:17).

What he perceived in the Temple becomes clearer in verses 18-27. He perceived two great truths: The prosperity of the wicked is only temporary, and closeness to God is the greatest good for humans. His intellectual confusion turned into religious hope when he recognized more profoundly than ever before that God is near and that God is the only secure refuge. Now his task is to tell others about these two great insights.

The "solution" (if one can call it that) in Psalm 73 to the problem posed by the prosperity of the wicked is not far from that found in the book of Job. There, too, Job undergoes a spiritual "conversion" of perspective (see Job 42:1-6) and comes to view the world from God's perspective rather than from his own narrow human view of retributive justice. Later Jewish and early Christian writers found what they regarded as an even more satisfactory approach with their belief in life after death and the last judgment according to one's deeds during life on earth. However, in the present the psalmist's experience of God's nearness to us, and especially the beautiful image of God taking us by the hand as a parent leads, guides, and protects a young child, is perhaps the best image of hope for us as we make our way through life in a world where the wicked still too often seem to prosper.

Questions: Does the image of God holding your right hand give you new hope? Why? Does the psalmist's insight into God's closeness put the law of retribution into a new perspective for you?

24. The Divine Warrior (Psalm 76)

> *"But you indeed are awesome! Who can stand before you*
> *when once your anger is roused?"* (Ps 76:7)

To many persons today the idea of God as a warrior is foreign and repugnant. That was not the case in biblical times. One of the very early parts of the Hebrew Bible, the Song of Moses at the Reed Sea in Exodus 15, proclaims, "The Lord is a warrior; the Lord is his name" (15:3). Near the end of the New Testament,

John the Seer describes the risen Christ as a warrior riding on a white horse, and writes "in righteousness he judges and makes war" (Rev 19:11).

Before dismissing such symbolism as outdated and naive, we need to recall that these images are the statements of an embattled people's total reliance on God rather than on themselves. The language of the book of Psalms is not that of the physical sciences, philosophy, or systematic theology. It is the language of the imagination and of hope (poetry). And of course, as we have seen throughout this book, the divine warrior is only one image of God among the many in the book of Psalms. Given the situations of ancient Israel in Egypt (slaves) and the early Christians addressed in Revelation (facing the prospect of martyrdom), the divine warrior was an image of hope for oppressed and depressed persons. It speaks to our recurrent hopes for a champion or savior in hard times.

Psalm 76 is a song of Zion, in praise of the Jerusalem Temple as God's dwelling place. It describes how Yahweh, the God of Israel, took up residence on Mount Zion. In doing so it appeals to the Exodus event as a pattern for his victory and evokes the words of the Song of Moses, "The Lord is a warrior." After identifying Mount Zion as God's abode (76:1-3), it describes the "military" exploits of the glorious and awesome divine warrior (76:4-10). Then in verses 11-12 it invites others to pay him homage at the Temple.

In verses 1-3 the psalmist glorifies Zion in Judah where God is known and acknowledged, and where he is especially present. The name "Salem" has some connection with Jerusalem and also with the Hebrew word for "peace" (*shalom*). In verse 3 the psalmist insists that Zion came to be Yahweh's dwelling place through his activity as a powerful warrior who destroyed the weapons (arrows, shields, swords, etc.) of his enemies. Here the triumph is not attributed to David as it is in 2 Samuel 5:6-10. In fact, David's capture of Jerusalem is recounted there with remarkable restraint, as if there were not much of a battle at all. Here the psalmist awards the victory totally to Yahweh the divine warrior and describes it in terms reminiscent of Yahweh's victory over the Egyptians at the Reed Sea.

The central part (76:4-10) of this song of Zion celebrates the exploits of the "glorious" and "awesome" divine warrior. His victory over his enemies (and Israel's enemies) is effortless and complete. His chief weapon is his word; at his rebuke "both rider and horse lay stunned" (76:6). And his goal is noble: "to save all the oppressed of the earth" (76:9). Rather than being annoyed or scandalized by the image of the divine warrior, we need to look beneath it and see what hopes it arouses. The image looks forward to the intervention of an all-powerful savior or champion in the midst of an apparently hopeless situation. The divine warrior is one who will triumph by word alone, and will vindicate poor and oppressed people.

The proper response (76:11-12) to the exploits of the divine warrior is fear in the sense of showing proper respect to the glorious and awesome one. The epithet "awesome" (76:7, 11) is based on the Hebrew verb to "fear" (*yarah*). The psalmist invites his listeners to "make vows," that is, to promise to offer sacrifices to the God whose earthly dwelling is preeminently at the Jerusalem Temple, and to carry out those vows by offering their sacrifices there. The awesome one in turn inspires fear among the kings of the earth. The theme of the divine warrior is linked with those of Mount Zion as his abode and Yahweh as the real king in Israel and in all the world.

The portrayal of the risen Jesus as the divine warrior appears only in Revelation 19:11-16. His arrival marks the beginning of the unfolding of the great events that will issue in the emergence of the New Jerusalem. He is clothed in a white robe "dipped in blood" (symbolizing the atoning value of his death on the cross), and "his name is called the Word of God" (19:13). In Ephesians 6:10-20 the good Christian is portrayed as the soldier of Jesus Christ. Here it is important to look carefully at this soldier's weapons. They are truth, righteousness, the Gospel of peace, faith, salvation, and the word of God. These are no ordinary soldiers. Rather, they are the servants of the divine warrior, the glorious and awesome one, who takes the side of the poor and oppressed.

Questions: Does the image of God as a warrior comfort or repel you? How does the divine warrior differ from human warriors? How do you feel about applying this image to Jesus?

25. THE DIVINE ASSEMBLY (PSALM 82)

> *"God has taken his place in the divine council;*
> *in the midst of the gods he holds judgment."* (Ps 82:1)

One of the most persistent images in the ancient Near Eastern texts discovered in recent centuries is the council or assembly of the gods. Most of the peoples then were polytheists who envisioned their many gods functioning in heaven in a kind of primitive democracy. As in most democracies, there were tales of struggles for power and leadership, with the strongest and wisest god emerging as the victor.

The idea of the assembly of the gods made its way into the Old Testament as in 1 Kings 22:19-22 and Isaiah 6:1-13 and 40:1-9. Israel itself was slow to come to the concept of one God only (monotheism). Before the exile to Babylon in the sixth century B.C.E. most ancient Israelites were henotheists, that is, accepting a multiplicity of gods but believing that their national god, Yahweh, possessed the power and preeminence of the Most High God. Their neighbors probably held similar views about their own national gods.

Ancient Israel's transition from henotheism to monotheism appears most decisively in Isaiah 40–55, the part of the book written around 537 B.C.E., to encourage the exiles in Babylon to return to Jerusalem and start over again. There Yahweh asserts, "I am He; I am the first, and I am the last" (Isa 48:12). The gods of other nations are dismissed as lifeless idols. It is paradoxical that at one of the lowest points in their history ancient Israelites affirmed that their national god is the one and only true God.

Psalm 82 must be read against this ancient Near Eastern background. It celebrates the kingship of Yahweh. It takes for granted the presence of other gods in the divine assembly and explains why they were not on the same level as Israel's Lord. It also proposes to describe why and how these gods lost their status as gods by becoming mortal. The result of this session of the council of the gods described in Psalm 82 is that only Yahweh, the God of Israel, remains the ground of hope for all who seek justice.

The psalm purports to describe a trial taking place in heaven at an assembly of the gods. In this trial Yahweh functions as prosecutor, judge, and jury. The psalm reports on the trial (82:1-5) and the verdict (82:6-7), and closes with a comment by the psalmist (82:8).

The account of the trial (82:1-5) contains a description of the scene (82:1), the charge (82:2-4), and a comment either by the psalmist or Yahweh (82:5). The Most High God presides. His charge is that the other gods have judged humans unjustly and have shown favor to the wicked. The assumption behind the charge is that the gods have the power and duty to regulate the lives of humans in ways that are just. However, the justice that Yahweh envisions is weighted toward protecting the most vulnerable in human society. That point is underlined by the use of five synonyms for such persons in the indictment: "weak," "orphan," "lowly," "destitute," and "needy." The charge is that these gods have failed to carry out their duties in monitoring and enforcing justice among humans. The comment in verse 5 suggests that in the last analysis these gods are ignorant, confused, powerless, and generally useless. No one should hope in them for help.

The verdict (82:6-7) is the demotion of these gods to the human level. In ancient Near Eastern mythology, what set the gods apart from humankind was their immortality. While acknowledging their divinity ("You are gods"), Yahweh passes a death sentence on them: "you shall die like mortals." The final comment (82:8) asks that the only God still remaining in the divine assembly, the one to whom all the nations belong, take the place of the demoted gods and serve as the just judge in human affairs. Thus he is asked to insure that God's will might be done on earth as it is done in heaven.

In John 10:34-35 Jesus deflects the criticism that he has made himself God by citing Psalm 82:6 ("You are gods"). However, through his resurrection Jesus has gained precisely what the gods in Psalm 82 have lost: immortality. Through the risen Jesus humans can in turn hope to enjoy the privilege of immortality. In Revelation 4–5 the image of the divine council reappears, and the risen Christ alone is found worthy to open the scroll describing what will be. The risen Christ will then enforce divine justice among humans on earth, with particular attention to vindicating those most in need of justice, that is, those suffering for their fidelity to the one and only God.

Questions: How does the ancient image of the assembly of the gods fit with your image of God? Why and for whom does Yahweh emerge as the one and only God? Why is Yahweh alone worthy of trust and hope?

26. DARKNESS (PSALM 88)

> *"You have put me in the depths of the Pit,*
> *in the regions dark and deep."* (Ps 88:6)

How deep into the darkness of suffering can one go? What happens when God seems to be absent? What happens when God seems to be the cause of the suffering? Where does hope come in? These are the hard questions raised by Psalm 88, which is known as the gloomiest psalm.

Psalm 88 is generally classified as a lament. It features many direct addresses to God, complaints about the present situation, and petitions to God to do something on the psalmist's behalf. There are hardly any expressions of trust in God and no indication that the situation has been resolved. Rather, it ends on a note of "darkness." Indeed, the image of darkness (see 88:6, 13, 18) is one of the themes that unify the composition.

Psalm 88 consists of a first round of complaints (88:1-9a), reasons why God should alleviate the psalmist's sufferings (88:9b-12), and a second round of complaints (88:13-18). Each of the three parts begins with an address to God ("O Lord"), a reference to time, and the psalmist's protestation of prayer ("I cry out"). The psalm has sometimes been described as a dialogue with an absent God. In the final analysis, however, God is somehow present in the midst of all the darkness, at least present enough to be engaged on a personal level. And that is where the hope can be found.

The first round of complaints (88:1-9a) indicates that the situation was serious and even life-threatening. This part of the psalm is important for understanding how ancient Israelites, especially before the Exile, envisioned life after death. They imagined that after death the spirit of the person went to Sheol, a place more like limbo than heaven or hell. In verses 4-6 Sheol is called variously "the Pit," the place of the dead, "the depths," and "the regions dark and deep." Sheol was not a place to which someone would normally want to go (but see Job 3:11-19).

In verses 7-9a the psalmist blames God for his troubles. In many laments the psalmist points to his "enemies" and asks God to defeat and put them to shame. Here, however, the psalmist points the finger of blame directly at God: "Your wrath lies heavy upon me." He holds God responsible not only for his near-fatal suffering but also for the alienation and loneliness that he is experiencing as a result. But God is not totally absent. Rather, the psalmist senses God's presence at least enough to make his accusations against God. He is not an atheist or an agnostic.

In the part devoted to reasons why God should act now (88:9b-12), the psalmist claims that he calls on the Lord every day, and reminds God that nothing will be gained from his death. In fact, it is in God's best interests to save him. Here he adds another list of synonyms for Sheol: the place of the "shades" (like ghosts), "Abaddon" (the place of loss and destruction), "the darkness," and "the land of forgetfulness." In the form of six rhetorical questions, the psalmist observes that the inhabitants of Sheol are oblivious to the mighty acts of God and therefore cannot praise God for them.

The second round of complaints (88:13-18) begins again with an address ("O LORD"), a time reference ("morning"), and another word of protest ("I cry out to you"). A note of hope creeps into verse 14. The psalmist suggests that if God stopped hiding his face, the psalmist might be well again. But the hope is fleeting, and the psalmist reverts to blaming God ("Your wrath has swept over me") and to bemoaning his loneliness ("my companions are in darkness").

The inclusion of this gloomy psalm in the canonical Scriptures of Israel and of the church is a ray of hope for suffering persons. It is all right to complain about suffering; it is all right to rail at God; and you are not alone in your suffering and depression. This psalm can help us all confront the grim reality of suffering and the terrifying experience of God's apparent absence when God's help is needed most. Nevertheless, the apparently absent God is present enough to be addressed in prayer, to be criticized, and to be the object of anger.

Even though the psalmist feels that God has given up on him, he refuses to give up on God. It is relatively easy to believe in God when things are going well for us and life proceeds in an orderly way. In Psalm 88, however, the psalmist's life is a mess and God seems far away. By challenging God and expressing anger at God, the psalmist is able to express at least a glimmer of hope in the midst of great suffering.

In dealing with Psalm 22 which begins, "My God my God, why have you forsaken me?" I insisted that one must read the whole psalm, including the vindication and thanksgiving that come at the end. The whole psalm catches nicely the dynamic of the paschal mystery of Jesus' passion, death, and resurrection. Nevertheless, this interpretation does not deny that Jesus meant what he said in the first part of the psalm. That is, Jesus may well have experienced some of the darkness that comes with intense suffering described so effectively in Psalm 88.

Questions: Have you ever found yourself in spiritual darkness and without hope? Did it help to pray? How do you understand life after death?

27. ABIDING IN GOD (PSALM 91)

"You who live in the shelter of the Most High,
who abide in the shadow of the Almighty." (Ps 91:1)

Do you trust God? That has been described as the most fundamental question of the spiritual life. For many people today God is not much of a factor in their lives. Even those who are believers may think of God as abstract and distant, and doubt God's personal care for them. Others fear that God may be deceiving them, or is all too ready to punish them, or will desert them when they are in need. The Bible, however, portrays God as both merciful and just, as one who wants the best for those who love him, as one who can and should be trusted. Those who trust this God can hope in God.

Abiding is one of the most prominent biblical terms associated with trust in God. The Hebrew and Greek words can also be translated "remain," "lodge," or "dwell." The image evokes a peaceful, confident, and enduring relationship with God, like that one might have with a loving parent or spouse or friend. Those who abide in God trust God and therefore can and do hope in God. Trust is fundamental to hope.

Psalm 91 is a psalm of trust. It consists of three series of promises of divine protection and security (91:1-8, 9-13, 14-16). The psalmist is the speaker in the first two series, while in the third series God speaks in first-person language.

The first series (91:1-8) begins with an address to those who abide in God. It employs several of the images that are commonly used in the psalms to describe trust in God: "the shelter of the Most High," "the shadow of the Almighty," "refuge," and "fortress." While some interpreters restrict these images to the Jerusalem Temple, most take them as referring more generally to God. The first set of images depicting the reasons why one should trust God (91:3-4b) has to do with birds. God promises to preserve those who abide in him from the traps of hunters, and to protect them like an eagle protecting its young by flying high above the earth (see Exod 19:4; Deut 32:11). In a second set of images (91:4c-8) concerning warfare, God's faithfulness is compared to a large shield protecting those who abide in him. At all times—day and night, darkness and noonday—God exercises constant vigilance on behalf of those who trust him. The image of their being so protected in battle that they can be spectators at the defeat of the wicked (91:7-8) evokes what happened during the exodus from Egypt (see Exod 14:13-14).

The second series (91:9-13) begins as the first series did, with the divine titles "Lord" and "the Most High" and the images of refuge and dwelling place. It first promises protection from harm and from every "scourge," perhaps a plague or "pestilence" as in verse 6. Then it enlists the angels as helpers in providing protection for those who trust God, thus evoking passages like Exodus 23:20, 23, and 32:34 (see also Matt 4:6 and Luke 4:10-11 where the passage is quoted in the account of Jesus' temptation). Finally it promises that those who abide in God will suffer no harm from lions and adders and will even be able to trample them underfoot without harm.

In the third (and shortest) series (91:14-16) the role of the speaker shifts from the psalmist to God speaking in the first-person singular ("I"). Here the promises are made to "those who love me," a synonym for those who abide in God. The many verbs used in the divine oracle—"deliver," "protect," "answer," "be with," "rescue," "honor," "satisfy," and "show salvation"— express various facets of God's loving care for those who abide and trust in God.

Psalm 91 offers many promises of protection and security. These promises seem to involve a circular or spiraling relationship between those who abide in God and God's care for them. The promises do not necessarily guarantee a life without problems or sufferings. What they do promise in the last analysis is that God will be present to those who remain present to him. In the relationship of mutual abiding there will be such a foundation of trust that whatever problems and sufferings do emerge will not destroy what is most basic in the spiritual life: right relationship with God.

The theme of abiding in God is developed in Jesus' farewell discourse in John 15. There he describes the relationship with God made possible through his life, death, and resurrection for those who believe and live. The Father, Jesus, and those who follow him exist in a kind of chain of love: "As the Father has loved me, so I have loved you; abide in my love" (John 15:9). The task of those who abide in love is to "bear fruit," that is, in believing, loving, and doing good deeds. They can be confident that what they seek in prayer will be granted to them, perhaps along the lines of the protection and security promised in Psalm 91. The result of their abiding in God's love revealed through Jesus the Word of God will be perfect joy. This relationship of abiding is the proper context for Christian hope.

Questions: What is the effect of the different images to describe abiding in God? Which ones are most comforting to you? What is the connection between abiding and hoping?

28. TODAY (PSALM 95)

"O that today you would listen to his voice!" (Ps 95:7)

Don't put off until tomorrow what you can do today. That is wise advice. As the maxim suggests, it is usually better to seize the moment as it presents itself and do what needs to be done while it is still possible. Hopeful persons are neither presumptuous nor despairing. Presumptuous persons assume that God or someone else will "take care" of them and are content to do nothing. Despairing persons have no hope because they cannot imagine a future different from the present evil situation. By contrast, hopeful persons try to discern what God might be saying to them in the present moment and to act appropriately by way of response.

"Today" is a prominent word in Psalm 95. It marks the sharp and somewhat awkward transition between the two invitations to worship God (95:1-5, 6-7c) and the exhortation to avoid the rebelliousness shown by the exodus generation (95:7d-11). Psalm 95 seems to have been connected with the celebration of the kingship of Yahweh, as its proximity and similarity to Psalms 93, 96, 97, 98, and 99 suggest. The exhortation, which may at one point have been a separate piece, underscores the need for those who honor Yahweh as king to respond with reverence and obedience.

The first invitation begins in verses 1-2 with four calls to sing the praises ("sing," "make a joyful noise," "thanksgiving," "make a joyful noise") of God who is "the rock of our salvation." That image of God combines the idea of God as stable and solid (and so to be trusted) with his saving actions (the one who saves) on behalf of God's people and all creation. One reason why God's praises should be sung is given in verses 3-5. Here Yahweh is described as "a great God, and a great King above all gods," thus alluding to ancient Israel's belief that its God reigns supreme in the divine assembly. The great King is praised especially for his work of creation. The two pairs—depths of the earth and heights of the mountains, and the sea and the dry land—take in all of the cosmos.

A second and shorter invitation to praise God begins in verse 6 with a call to approach God with reverent and respectful gestures: "bow down . . . kneel." Here God is praised as "our Maker." The reason why God should be praised according to verse 7a concerns the personal relationship with Israel as God's people. As in Psalm 23, the Lord is depicted with the image of the shepherd and God's people are portrayed as the flock that is especially dear to him as he is its shepherd.

The exhortation in verses 7d-11 begins with a plea to listen to God's word and to act upon it "today." Then moving back in time to the Exodus generation during their wanderings in the wilderness, it recalls their rebellion against Moses and God described in Exodus 17:1-7. That rebellion took place at Meribah and Massah, which are Hebrew words for "strife" and "testing," respectively. The quarrel was precipitated by the lack of water available for the people in the wilderness of Sinai. There the people lost hope in God's ability and willingness to provide for them. The crisis was resolved miraculously when Moses was told by God to strike a rock at Mount Horeb and abundant waters flowed out from it. Because of their rebelliousness most of the people in the exodus generation (including Moses) were not allowed to enter the Promised Land. In this context God's "rest" refers to the land of Canaan.

The calls to worship God as king and the exhortation to listen to him "today" do not fit together smoothly in tone and content. However, their present juxtaposition has the effect of insisting that when approaching God in worship, God's people must be willing to hear and obey ("listen to his voice") what the great King requires. They must avoid repeating the negative example of rebelliousness displayed by the Exodus generation. Here again the Exodus serves as the paradigm or pattern for "today," even when the example is negative and not to be repeated, in every generation. Rather than repeating the disobedience of the past (despair) or putting off obedience to God to the distant future (presumption), the psalmist insists that "today" is the proper moment to worship God as the great King and to act with respect and obedience toward him as Creator and loving Shepherd.

The exhortation in Psalm 95:7d-11 is quoted and interpreted in great detail in Hebrews 3:7–4:11. There "rest" is understood to be the eternal life with God made possible through Jesus' death and resurrection. The early Christians (like their Israelite predecessors) are challenged to reject the bad example displayed by the wandering people of God and instead to hear and act upon the word of God "today," while the promise of entering

God's rest is still open. The Christians addressed in Hebrews seem to have been wavering in their faith in Jesus and in their allegiance to the Christian community. In response, the author of Hebrews insists that they must make a decision "today" for Jesus as "the pioneer and perfecter of our faith" (Heb 12:2). His message is, Don't put off until tomorrow what you do today. Hopeful persons are willing and able to hear God's voice "today" and act upon it.

Questions: How does hope differ from presumption and despair? How do you understand the image of "rest"? How is "today" an image of hope?

29. THE MERCIFUL ONE (PSALM 103)

"The LORD is merciful and gracious,
slow to anger and abounding in steadfast love." (Ps 103:8)

Whom do you trust? In whom (or what) do you hope? The many images of hope treated thus far in this book show repeatedly that the psalmists of ancient Israel put their trust and hope in Yahweh, the God of Israel. He was their king, shepherd, rock, refuge, and so many other things. But what kind of God is he? What are the most prominent characteristics of the God of Israel, the one whom Christians worship as the Father of our Lord Jesus Christ?

Many people persist in contrasting the wrathful God of the Old Testament and the loving God of the New Testament. Such persons have not read Psalm 103 (or most of the Old Testament either). This psalm is a hymn in praise of God's mercy and graciousness. It is a commentary on the definition of God revealed to Moses in Exodus 34:6 and repeated in Psalm 103: "The LORD is merciful and gracious, slow to anger and abounding in steadfast love."

Psalm 103 begins (103:1-2) and ends (103:20-22) with repeated calls to bless the Lord. The first part (103:1-14) describes God's mercy and graciousness in dealing with individuals (103:1-5) and with God's people (103:6-14). The second part (103:15-22) contrasts earthly beings and God (103:15-18) and celebrates God's sovereignty over heavenly beings (103:19-22).

Psalm 103 begins (103:1-2) with the psalmist calling upon himself ("my soul") to bless God for who God is ("his holy name") and for what God does for us ("all his benefits"). The latter point prompts a list of the good things (103:3-5) that God does for individuals. God forgives their sins, heals their sicknesses, saves them from death ("the Pit"), shows them love and mercy, gives them good gifts, and bestows health and happiness upon them. Many interpreters suppose that in verse 3 the psalmist has linked sin and sickness. However, it is not necessary to find a causal connection between them here or to interpret the whole list as applying to physical healing.

In verses 6-14 the psalmist moves from the benefits that God grants to individuals to what God does for the people as a nation. What leads the list is "justice for all who are oppressed" (103:6). The core of this part of Psalm 103 is the quotation of Exodus 34:6: "The Lord is merciful and gracious." The justice of God here and elsewhere in the Bible is not strict retributive justice ("an eye for an eye"). Rather, God's mercy overrides or trumps God's justice, according to verses 9-10. The God of the Bible, the one in whom the psalmist trusts and hopes, abounds in "steadfast love" (*hesed* in Hebrew). This term has as its context God's covenant relationship with Israel as his people. The greatness of God's steadfast love surpasses anything in the heavens or on earth. The best analogy is the love that good parents show to their children. Moreover, the compassionate God has sympathy for us precisely because he knows that "we are dust" (103:14).

Taking its starting point from the end of verse 14 ("we are dust"), the second part of Psalm 103 contrasts the transitory character of human existence with the eternal character of God's justice and mercy. In verses 15-16 various images—grass, flowers, and wind—indicate the transience of humankind, while in verses 17-18 God's steadfast love is described as everlasting and his justice carries on for generations on behalf of those who remain faithful to the stipulations of his covenant.

The final section (103:19-22) moves from the earthly realm to the heavenly realm where God "rules over all." The psalm closes with four calls to "bless the LORD," addressed first to heavenly beings (angels, mighty ones, his ministers), then to all God's works in creation, and finally back to the psalmist ("Bless the LORD, O my soul"). These calls affirm the sovereignty of God over all creation.

Whom do you trust? In whom (or what) do you hope? The portrait of God presented in Psalm 103 can and does elicit trust and hope. It has been correctly said that the two great themes of the Bible are the mercy and justice of God. The mercy of God is evident to those who know and love God. And the justice of God is tempered by mercy. Christians believe that Jesus as the Word of God incarnated those two great attributes of God ("grace and truth came through Jesus Christ," John 1:17), especially in his teaching, healing, and caring for the "lost sheep" among God's people. His example challenges his followers to show mercy and justice to others.

Questions: Have you been a recipient of mercy from God? Did it make you more hopeful? Do you see any contradiction between God's mercy and justice?

30. THE SAVIOR (PSALM 106)

> *"Save us, O LORD our God,*
> *and gather us from among the nations,*
> *that we may give thanks to your holy name*
> *and glory in your praise."* (Ps 106:47)

The God who is the main character in the Psalms is not an abstract or distant figure. Rather, Yahweh enters into the lives of individuals and especially into the life of his chosen people. He tries to guide his people along right paths. He cares for them and is willing to forgive them when they stray. At many points in his people's history God alone was able to "save" them, that is, rescue them from some crisis and enable them to start afresh. Throughout the Psalms Yahweh appears as Israel's Savior because he saved Israel repeatedly in the past (especially in the Exodus) and shows himself willing and able to save them in the present and future. God the Savior is the ground of the people's hope and the reason why they can continue to hope for the future.

Psalm 106 is generally classified as a historical psalm, that is, a recital of episodes in ancient Israel's history and God's perceived role in them. Other examples of the historical psalms include Psalms 78, 105, 135, and 136. This historical psalm reflects on seven episodes in Israel's history (106:7-12, 13-15, 16-18, 19-23, 24-31, 32-33, and 34-46) in which Israel went astray and was saved only by its merciful and gracious God. The introduction (106:1-6) and the conclusion (106:47) place the historical recital in the context of a prayer, something like a lament. The concluding doxology (106:48) rounds off book 4, and was not originally part of Psalm 106.

The petition in verse 47 ("gather us from among the nations") suggests that Psalm 106 was composed during the Babylonian exile in the sixth century B.C.E. In a situation in which Yahweh's people seemed to have no future at all, their only hope was that God might forgive their sins and save them as he had done often in the past. The word "save" applied to God appears not only in verse 47 but also in verses 8, 10, and 21. Without the saving power of God, there was no hope for Israel in exile.

The introduction (106:1-6) consists of a call to praise and thank God, a question and answer about who can recite the mighty acts of God, a petition to God to act on Israel's behalf, and a confession of the people's sins. What the psalmist hopes for his people in exile (see v. 5) is their renewed prosperity and happiness, so that they may once again glory in their heritage as God's chosen people.

The seven episodes that are recounted in the body of the psalms do not concern Israel's triumphs or finest hours. Rather, they deal with the people's sins and God's willingness to show mercy and to save them. Since the Exile was interpreted as God's just punishment for the people's sins, the effect of the recital is to remind God that in the past God's practice has been to show mercy and save his people despite their sins.

The seven episodes treat various moments in ancient Israel's history. (1) Verses 7-12: At the Re(e)d Sea (see Exod 14) the people rebelled against the Most High. Nevertheless, God saved them (106:8, 10) from their Egyptian enemies and led them across safely. (2) Verses 13-15: In the wilderness (see Num 11) the people had a craving for meat and so put God to the test. God sent them quails along with a disease as punishment for their lack of trust in him. (3) Verses 16-18: In the camp (see Num 16) there was a rebellion against Moses and Aaron. Although the rebel leaders were punished, most of the people were spared. (4) Verses 19-23: At Mount Horeb (see Exod 32–34) where the people worshiped the golden calf instead of the God who had saved them, God accepted Moses' prayer and did not destroy the people. (5) Verses 24-31: When the people worshiped the pagan god known as the Baal of Peor (see Num 13–14, and 25) God punished them with a plague that ceased only when Phinehas arose and interceded with God as Moses had done previously. (6) Verses 32-33: At Meribah (see Exod 17:1-7) the people rebelled against Moses and angered God. (7) Verses 34-36: In the land of Canaan Israel too often adopted the religious practices of the native people (even to the point of child sacrifice). The psalmist traces the Exile to these sins. Nevertheless, he retains the hope that God the Savior will hear the people's cries. This hope is based on how in the past God remembered the covenant and showed compassion to the people. The basic reason for the psalmist's hope is "the abundance of [God's] steadfast love" (106:45).

The ground of ancient Israel's hope was the God who saves. That characteristic of the God of the Bible is echoed in the name of Jesus, which is a form of Joshua. As Matthew explains, the name given to Jesus of Nazareth was very appropriate to his mission, since it means "he will save his people from their sins" (Matt 1:21). The name of Jesus is an apt summary of Psalm 106.

Questions: What enabled Israel in exile to continue hoping in Yahweh? What did salvation mean to them? What does it mean to you?

31. MELCHIZEDEK (PSALM 110)

"The LORD has sworn and will not change his mind,
'You are a priest forever according to the order of Melchizedek.'"
(Ps 110:4)

In the Bible Melchizedek is a shadowy figure from the early days of Israel's history as the people of God. That history began in Genesis 12 with God's call to Abraham to leave his homeland and become the progenitor of a great nation. In Genesis 14:18-20 Melchizedek appears out of nowhere when he brings bread and wine to Abraham, blesses Abraham, and receives a tenth of Abraham's share of the spoils from battle. He is identified as the king of Salem (perhaps a form of the name Jerusalem) and a "priest of the Most High God." Through that text and the only other Old Testament reference to him in Psalm 110:4, Melchizedek has become an image of hope for Jews and Christians.

Psalm 110 is a royal psalm (like Psalm 2), and was perhaps composed for the coronation of a king or for the anniversary of a coronation. Since the king was "anointed," it can also be called a messianic psalm. It consists of two statements or oracles attributed to the Lord (Yahweh) in verses 1 and 4, along with developments of each oracle in verses 2-3 and 5-7, respectively. The psalm is royal in a double sense, in that it links God's kingship with the Davidic monarchy. It asserts that the heavenly king works through the earthly king, and vice versa.

The first oracle (110:1) comes from "the LORD" (Yahweh) to "my lord" (the king). God invites the king to take a seat at his right hand and promises to subject the king's enemies to him (as his footstool). In the development of the oracle (110:2-3) the psalmist has the Lord providing the dynamism to make the king into a powerful warrior against his enemies, to enable him to attract a large force of volunteers, to lead those armies in battle beginning from God's holy mountain (Zion), and to retain the health and vigor of his youth. It is through Yahweh's help that the earthly king will achieve all his success.

In the second oracle (110:4) the Lord (Yahweh) swears to the king that the king will be "a priest forever according to the order of Melchizedek." That statement needs some historical background. Jerusalem became the capital of the confederacy of the twelve tribes of Israel only under King David. Since Jerusalem did not belong to the territory of any one tribe, it could serve as a unifying principle for all the tribes (like Washington, DC, in the United States). David captured Jerusalem, set up his residence there, and planned to build a temple to Yahweh. He also used local traditions about Melchizedek, the priest king of Salem, to smooth out the city's transition from being a Canaanite-Jebusite stronghold to being the capital for the twelve tribes of Israel. Like other ancient Near Eastern kings, David and Solomon sometimes performed "priestly" functions.

The oracle in Psalm 110:4 links the king in David's line with Melchizedek and Yahweh with the Most High God. In the development in verses 5-7 the Lord promises to fight the king's battles and to rout his enemies. Behind the lurid descriptions of the Lord's victories is the image of the divine warrior and the connections between the heavenly king and the earthly king. The final verse (110:7) remains a textual puzzle. Perhaps the idea is something like that of verse 3, that is, the wish that the king may enjoy good health and happiness.

Psalm 110 is "messianic" in the most basic sense that it may well have accompanied the anointing of the new king. It also put forward an ideal of perfect symbiosis between divine rule and human kingship in Israel. But at least according to the books of Samuel and Kings, very few of the historical kings in Judah and Israel came close to fulfilling that ideal. Thus the mysterious Melchizedek provided an image of hope for a future truly righteous king in Israel.

The author of the letter to the Hebrews found in Melchizedek a type of the royal priesthood of Jesus Christ. As a member of the tribe of Judah and a legal descendant of King David, Jesus could not qualify to be a member of the Levitical priesthood in Israel. The theological thesis of Hebrews is that Jesus was both the perfect sacrifice for sins and the great high priest because he willingly offered himself in sacrifice. From the references to Melchizedek in Genesis 14:18-20 and Psalm 110:4 the author of Hebrews argued that Jesus was the ideal priest-king according to the "order" or pattern of Melchizedek, and was therefore the fulfillment of Israel's hopes for the ideal priest-king in perfect harmony with the Most High God.

Questions: How did the figure of Melchizedek come to function in Israel's hopes for an ideal king? How did Melchizedek become a type of Jesus the great high priest? How could Jesus be called a priest?

32. Fear of the Lord (Psalm 111)

> *"The fear of the LORD is the beginning of wisdom;*
> *all those who practice it have a good understanding.*
> *His praise endures forever."* (Ps 111:10)

In the Psalms (and the rest of the Bible too), "fear of the LORD" is not a bad thing. We need to rid ourselves of images of fear of the Lord as hiding from God or cowering in a corner because we think that God is going to strike us down. Rather, fear of the Lord is the wise and proper response to who God is and what God has done, and who we are before God.

In many ancient Near Eastern and Old Testament texts, fear of the Lord is a respectful response to the order that God has imposed upon the cosmos and brought about in the moral, religious, and social spheres of human life. Those who fear the Lord recognize that divinely imposed order and try to integrate themselves into it. Fear of the Lord is knowing one's place in God's universe, and therefore is the beginning of real wisdom. Those who fear God are respectful and submissive toward God, and gladly take upon themselves the duty to worship God in prayer and good works.

Psalm 111 is the first in a series of several psalms devoted to praising God. It has elements of a thanksgiving ("I will give thanks to the LORD," 111:1), suggesting some kind of public testimony, perhaps in connection with a sacrifice offered at the Jerusalem Temple. It is an acrostic, consisting of twenty-two short units, each beginning with a successive letter in the Hebrew alphabet. The acrostic form contributes to the impression of completeness or comprehensiveness. Each short unit is made up of three or four Hebrew words.

The psalm begins and ends on a note of praise. The word "forever" and its synonyms run through the psalm (111:3, 5, 8, 9, 10). The key word, however, is "works" or "deeds" (see 111:2, 3, 4, 6, 7). According to Psalm 111, the "works of the LORD" provide the reason why one should "fear" God in the sense of awe in the presence of the Almighty. Only a God worthy of such awe can be the ground of hope.

What is striking about Psalm 111 is its appeal not to God's work of creation but rather to the mighty acts of God that constituted the pivotal events in the early history of Israel as God's people. The psalm consists of a call to praise and thank God (111:1-4), a recital of God's works on Israel's behalf (111:5-9), and a declaration that fear of the Lord is the beginning of wisdom (111:10).

The call to praise and thank God (111:1-4) assumes a communal setting. In the psalms the person who gives thanks bears witness to others regarding what God has done. Rather than describing a personal rescue or recovery, the psalmist here points to the "works of the LORD" and "his wonderful deeds." What these works are is anticipated by the familiar description of God as "merciful and gracious" from Exodus 34:6. The psalmist also calls attention to God's honor and majesty, as well as his righteousness in forming Israel into the people of God.

The formal recital of God's wonderful deeds (111:5-9) alludes to God's leading Israel out of slavery in Egypt, providing food for the wilderness generation, entering into a covenant relationship with Israel at Mount Sinai/Horeb, and bringing the people into the land of Canaan ("the heritage of the nations"). In verses 7-8 the psalmist describes God's works as "faithful and just," and praises his precepts as trustworthy, established forever, and to be put into practice. His testimony concludes with praise of God for redeeming his people and making an everlasting covenant with them. "Holy and awesome is his name" is an apt summary of Psalm 111.

The adjective "awesome" derives from the Hebrew root (*yarah*) meaning "fear." The proper response to the "awesome" one is fear of the Lord, which is in turn the beginning of wisdom. One can and should place one's trust and hope only in the awesome God who by his mighty acts made a group of slaves into a great people.

By his teaching and example Jesus taught all who follow him to approach God as a loving parent who deserves our respect, submission, and worship, that is, with fear of the Lord. In doing so he has expanded the scope of God's people beyond ethnic Israel. Moreover, he has taught us to approach God with confidence and hope because through him we know who God is and what God has done, and who we are before God. And so with proper respect and awe we too can address God as "Abba, Father." Fear of the Lord is not a bad thing.

Questions: How do you understand "fear of the LORD"? What is its connection with wisdom? How does it relate to hope?

33. THE KEEPER (PSALM 121)

"He who keeps Israel will neither slumber nor sleep." (Ps 121:4)

One of the several key words in Psalm 121 derives from the Hebrew root *shamar*. It means to "watch over, guard, preserve, and protect." In Psalm 121:4 the Lord (Yahweh) is called the one "who keeps Israel." This image can and should inspire trust, confidence, and hope in God, especially in the midst of a dangerous journey or some other crisis in life.

Psalm 121 is classified as a song of trust. It belongs to a group of fifteen psalms (120–134), each of which bears the superscription "a song of ascents." It is often said that these psalms were recited by pilgrims as they made their way through the mountainous countryside leading up to Jerusalem and its Temple. That suggestion fits well with Psalm 121 and several others in the block (but not all of them). Although more complicated proposals have been made about the songs of ascents, the pilgrimage hypothesis remains attractive. It certainly illumines the text of Psalm 121.

After a short dialogue (121:1-2), Psalm 121 moves in verses 3-8 into a description of the Lord (Yahweh) as the one who keeps Israel. The movement of the psalm is carried along by the words "help," "slumber," and "keep." It features such vivid images as slipping and shade. It begins and ends with the image of "coming" (121:1, 8).

In biblical times the journey up to Jerusalem would have been made primarily on foot, and the usual pathways would naturally attract bandits, as the parable of the Good Samaritan shows (see Luke 10:25-37). Those who made this dangerous journey did so in the hope that they would arrive and return safely.

In the dialogue (121:1-2) the most obvious scenario has the psalmist asking a question and answering it by himself. There may, however, be some ritual transaction or ceremony behind the dialogue. On the pilgrimage hypothesis for the songs of ascents, the "hills" would be the terrain leading up to and including the Jerusalem Temple. The dialogue has the effect of giving confidence to the pilgrims on the grounds that their help will certainly come from the Lord who created heaven and earth. That is a good reason for hope.

With the description of Yahweh as the keeper of Israel in verses 3-8 the psalm moves away from the dialogue format into the expository mode. For pilgrims making their way to Jerusalem on foot, a twisted ankle or some other physical injury would be disastrous. And sleeping at night could be very dangerous, due to animals, scorpions, or bandits. In verses 3-4 the psalmist assures the pilgrims that Yahweh will not allow their feet to slip or predators to harm them during sleep. The reason for such confidence is that the one "who keeps Israel neither slumbers nor sleeps."

Along the journey, according to verse 5, the Lord will be their "shade." The three great pilgrimage feasts in ancient Israel—Passover, Weeks/Pentecost, and Booths/Tabernacles— would generally occur when the chances of clouds or rain were slim. The intense Near Eastern sun could be very dangerous (dehydration, sunstroke, sunburn, etc.) to pilgrims out all day in the bright sunshine. But, according to verse 6, the protection offered by Yahweh will be constant, by sun and moon, and by day and night.

The final stanza (121:7-8) affirms that the one who keeps Israel will keep the travelers from all harm, and that this protection will last not only during the pilgrimage ("your going out and coming in") but also throughout the pilgrims' lives.

Psalm 121 is an appropriate text for anyone setting out on pilgrimage or some other dangerous journey. (Of course, every life is a pilgrimage of sorts.) One can imagine Jesus and his disciples reciting Psalm 121 as they made their way up to Jerusalem for the Passover celebration in 30 C.E. This psalm also illumines the parable of the Good Samaritan where the pilgrim is said to have fallen "into the hands of robbers, who stripped him, beat him, and went away, leaving him half dead" (Luke 10:30). Some church fathers interpreted the Good Samaritan as Jesus, and viewed the care exercised on behalf of the wounded man as symbolic of the care that God (and Jesus) shows to all kinds of people. As Psalm 121 affirms, the keeper of Israel is also the one "who made heaven and earth." This psalm can and should inspire trust, confidence, and hope in all of us who make the pilgrimage of life today in a very dangerous world.

Questions: Do you believe that God watches over and "keeps" you? Might you find Psalm 121 appropriate as you set out on a journey?

34. THE PEACE OF JERUSALEM (PSALM 122)

"Pray for the peace of Jerusalem:
'May they prosper who love you.'" (Ps 122:6)

If Psalm 121 gives us a sense of what it was like to make a pilgrimage to Jerusalem in biblical times, Psalm 122 tells us what it was like to arrive there and return home. It too belongs to the songs of ascents and comes to life when read in the context of a pilgrimage to Jerusalem.

Today Jerusalem is a place of deep controversy. It is sacred to Judaism, Christianity, and Islam. At different periods it has been controlled by each of the three monotheistic faiths. Today it remains one of the most disputed parcels of land in the world and one of the most neuralgic issues on the world political stage.

The etymology of Jerusalem is sometimes explained rather fancifully as "the city of peace." In biblical times Jerusalem was only rarely a city of peace. Around 1000 B.C.E. David captured Jerusalem from the Jebusites. Besides many sieges and battles throughout the centuries, it was destroyed almost entirely first in 587 B.C.E. by the Babylonians and then again in 70 C.E. by the Romans. Nevertheless, as people of hope we continue to pray for the peace of Jerusalem.

Psalm 122 is a song of Zion, like Psalms 46, 48, 76, 84, and 87. It first expresses the joy of pilgrims who had reached the goal of their pilgrimage in Jerusalem (122:1-5). Then it encourages pilgrims to continue praying for the peace of Jerusalem, and gives some sample prayers (122:6-9). As in Psalm 121, the movement of the psalm is carried along by key words: Jerusalem, tribes, thrones, peace, and "for the sake of."

In verses 1-2 the pilgrim expresses joy at having undertaken the pilgrimage and having arrived safely. He eagerly took up the suggestion, "Let us go to the house of the LORD." And he joyfully describes the experience of setting foot in Jerusalem, "Our feet are standing within your gates, O Jerusalem." One can often hear the same kind of enthusiasm from pilgrims and tourists today, who thrill to the experience of walking where David and Jesus once walked.

Was this the psalmist's first visit? Did he write the psalm then and there? Or was it composed after he returned home? These questions cannot be answered. But it can be said that wherever and whenever this psalm was composed, it retains the joy and enthusiasm of a pilgrim who has found what he was hoping for.

In verses 3-5 there is a description of Jerusalem's compact architecture ("bound firmly together"), as well as its functions as a religious center ("the tribes go up . . . to give thanks to the name of the LORD") and a government center ("there the thrones for judgment were set up").

Pilgrims inevitably go back home. The section about praying for the peace of Jerusalem (122:6-9) seems to reflect both the pilgrim's departure and a way of continuing the experience. In verses 6-7 there is a call to pray for the peace of Jerusalem, along with a sample prayer for its prosperity and security. The "walls" and "towers" refer to the massive exterior fortifications that provided the first line of defense against attackers. Then in verse 8 there is another invitation to pray, and another sample prayer, "Peace be within you," that is, in the interior spaces protected by the exterior walls and towers. Finally in verse 9 there is a promise to seek the good of Jerusalem especially because "the house of the LORD our God" is there.

The account of the boy Jesus in the Temple in Luke 2:41-52 captures some of the excitement and confusion that were part of pilgrimages to Jerusalem in biblical times. Even though Jesus seemed to be lost among the crowds, he was present in the Temple compound and engaged in dialogue with the Jewish teachers there. To his worried parents, he explained, "Did you not know that I must be in my Father's house?" (Luke 2:49).

Jerusalem today can be both exhilarating and depressing. It remains the site of many personal and political conflicts. That is why we today need to take up the challenge of Psalm 122, and hope and pray for the peace of Jerusalem.

Questions: Have you ever made a pilgrimage? Were your hopes fulfilled? Do you ever pray for the peace of Jerusalem?

35. WAITING (PSALM 130)

> *"I wait for the Lord, my soul waits,*
> *and in his word I hope."* (Ps 130:5)

Did you ever spend a whole day in an airport waiting for your airplane to take off and it never did? I once heard a flight attendant say that most of her life could be summed up with the words, "Hurry up and wait." Waiting can be hard.

Waiting and hoping are closely connected. The object of hope is something desirable and future. Hope whose object is already present is no longer hope. In all hoping there is an element of waiting, since the object is not yet here and in our grasp. In the Bible the object of hope is often God or dependent on God's action, and we cannot coerce God (try as we might). And so at the most important moments in our lives we often find ourselves waiting and hoping.

Psalm 130 is an individual lament. It is one of the seven penitential psalms, and is often referred to by the first two words in its Latin version, *De profundis*, which means "Out of the depths." It is addressed initially to the Lord and consists of complaints and petitions (130:1-3), an affirmation of trust in God (130:4-6), and an invitation to Israel to share in the psalmist's joy and hope (130:7-8).

The psalmist's complaints and petitions (130:1-3) are said to come "out of the depths." The Hebrew word here suggests that the depths of the sea are meant, and that the psalmist was near death by drowning. However, here the term may well be used in a metaphorical way to describe some other kind of crisis or even a deep depression. Whatever the precise cause may have been, the psalmist hopes that God will hear his prayers. He perceives some connection between his present plight and his own sin, and so is begging God for both forgiveness and rescue. He hopes that the forgiveness of his sin will bring about the resolution of the crisis.

In the affirmation of trust in God (130:4-6) the psalmist first (130:4) gives as a reason why God should forgive his sin and save him "so that you may be revered." The Hebrew word behind "revered" derives from the root for "fear." This is another indication that "fear of the LORD" refers to the respect and awe that God deserves. The psalmist here (as elsewhere) is suggesting that it is in God's own interest to forgive his sin, because that will increase God's honor and reputation.

The core verses of the psalm (130:5-6) use the rhetorical device of "step-parallelism." The two keywords "wait" and "hope" are linked, and the lead image of waiting is repeated and prolonged. The psalmist is waiting for a "word" from the Lord. This word is most likely some declaration of forgiveness and absolution, perhaps in the form of an oracle recited by a priest. In verse 6 the psalmist asserts that he awaits this word of forgiveness more eagerly than night-watchmen or soldiers on guard wait for morning to come. In a time before electricity the night was often regarded as a time of great terror and danger. The psalmist hopes fervently for God's word of forgiveness.

There is a sudden shift of tone in verses 7-8. As in many laments (most notably in Ps 22), one gets the impression that the crisis has been resolved; and now the psalmist is giving thanks to God for forgiveness and rescue by offering a sacrifice at the Jerusalem Temple, and inviting his family and friends to join in his celebration. It seems that he had received his word of forgiveness in some form, believed that God had absolved him from his sin, and now wants to tell all Israel about how his hope has been fulfilled. His waiting has been rewarded, and his hope has been realized. And so he wants others to share his experience, and to learn to wait and hope as he did. The ground of his (and their) hope is God's steadfast or covenant love (*ḥesed* in Hebrew) and God's power to "redeem" Israel from its sins.

Many early summaries of Christian faith interpreted Jesus' death as the one perfect sacrifice for sins and thus as the fulfillment of ancient Israel's hopes for forgiveness and redemption. For example, Paul quotes existing creedal statements to the effect that "Christ died for our sins in accordance with the scriptures" (1 Cor 15:3), and "God put forward [Jesus] as a sacrifice of atonement by his blood" (Rom 3:25). According to Mark 10:45, Jesus came "to give his life as a ransom for many." When these texts are read alongside Psalm 130, Jesus emerges as the long-awaited and hoped-for definitive word of forgiveness and absolution from God.

Questions: Why is waiting part of hoping? Do you see any link between suffering and sin? How do you regard the interpretation of Jesus' death as a sacrifice for sins?

36. HALLELUJAH (PSALM 135)

> *"For I know that the LORD is great;*
> *our LORD is above all gods."* (Ps 135:5)

"Hallelujah" is not a visual image. It does, however, often function as an oral-aural image. Most of us who say or sing "Hallelujah" have only a vague idea of its precise meaning. Yet it generally has the effect of expressing and increasing joy and hope in us. Historians of religion classify expressions like "Hallelujah" as a cultic cry.

"Hallelujah" is a combination of two Hebrew words. The first part is the second-person plural imperative of the verb "praise" (*halelu*), and the second part is a shortened form (*yah*) of the divine name "Yahweh." So the precise meaning of "Hallelujah" is "Praise the Lord."

Psalm 135 is a hymn of praise. It seems to have originated in connection with some form of temple liturgy. Its abundant use of phrases from early Old Testament traditions and certain late-Hebrew grammatical features suggest a relatively late date of composition. Such a dating fits with the monotheistic theology (Yahweh alone is God) in the psalm.

The material in Psalm 135 is arranged according to a concentric pattern:

A – a call to praise the Lord (135:1-4)

B – Yahweh's greatness revealed in creation (135:5-7)

C – Yahweh's greatness revealed in Israel's early history (135:8-14)

B – other gods are nothing (135:15-18)

A – a call to bless the Lord (135:19-21)

The expression "Hallelujah" (the NRSV translates it "Praise the LORD") begins and ends the psalm (135:1, 21). The reason for singing Yahweh's praises is to affirm that Yahweh alone is worthy of trust and hope.

The initial call to praise the Lord (135:1-4) is directed to Temple personnel or at least those present in the Jerusalem Temple complex. The reason why they should praise God is twofold: Yahweh is good and gracious, and Yahweh has chosen Israel as his people.

The recital of God's greatness in creation (135:5-7) suggests that in bringing order in heaven and on earth, and in controlling the elements, the Lord has shown himself to be "above all gods." That statement may seem like a remnant of ancient Near Eastern polytheism (many gods) or early biblical henotheism (Yahweh is supreme among the gods). In fact, the corresponding section (135:15-18) insists that the gods of other nations are nothing and so are not worthy of trust and hope.

At the center of Psalm 135 (vv. 8-14) is the account of Yahweh's greatness revealed in the events from the Exodus out of Egypt to the entrance into the Promised Land. These same events are the focus of the following hymn of praise (Ps 136) and appear throughout the book of Psalms as the basis for Israel's hopes in the future. As verses 13-14 suggest, because of Yahweh's glorious deeds on Israel's behalf in the past, there is now good reason to expect that he will vindicate and have compassion on his people in the future.

The polemic against idolatry (135:15-18) has many parallels in Isaiah 40–55 as well as the book of Wisdom, the letter of Jeremiah, and other early Jewish texts. In these texts there is no effort to understand the statues and other depictions of gods as symbols of divinity or aids to devotion. Instead the charge is that the idols have been created by human craftsmen and remain lifeless objects. They are not worthy of anyone's trust or hope.

The final call to bless the Lord (135:19-21) is directed to all Israel and especially to the priestly houses of Aaron and Levi, again indicating a connection with a temple liturgy. The final verse insists that the Lord who has shown his greatness in creation and in Israel's early history is the one whose earthly dwelling is the Jerusalem Temple.

In the Christian liturgical tradition the term "Hallelujah" is an especially appropriate response to Jesus' resurrection. Thus the Lord's act of power in raising Jesus from the dead at Easter is placed in the context of Yahweh's mighty acts in creation and in the early history of Israel. And the resurrection of Jesus in turn becomes the ground of our hope for resurrection and eternal life with God, as Paul argues in 1 Corinthians 15. The proper response is "Hallelujah."

Questions: For what actions do you praise God? Why do you praise God? Why has "Hallelujah" become associated especially with Easter?

37. THE RIVERS OF BABYLON (PSALM 137)

> *"By the rivers of Babylon—there we sat down and there we wept when we remembered Zion."* (Ps 137:1)

Hope often arises in the most desperate circumstances, when emotions run especially high. In the early sixth century B.C.E. the political and religious leaders of Judah were exiled to Babylon. Their exile followed the destruction of Jerusalem and its Temple dedicated to the worship of Yahweh. When the exiles arrived in Babylon, most of them seem to have ended up not in prisons but rather in something like refugee or settlement camps. Their major hope was to return home and resume their lives there. But that seemed very unlikely, even to them.

Psalm 137 can be classified as a lament, since there is a good deal of complaining about present sufferings. It has both communal and individual dimensions. It is the reverse of a song of Zion in that it concerns the absence of God and his people from Zion. It first describes the taunts that the exiles heard from their captors in Babylon (137:1-3). Then the psalmist pronounces a curse upon himself if he were ever to forget Jerusalem (137:4-6). It concludes with curses against Edom and Babylon (137:7-9), including what may be the most notorious verse in the Bible: "Happy shall they be who take your little ones and dash them against the rock!" (137:9). Psalm 137 shows that sometimes hope involves raw emotions and is not pretty.

The scene of the taunting (137:1-3) is set at the "rivers" or canals of Babylon, where the exiles had settled. As refugees usually do, they thought about going home, in this case to Jerusalem and Mount Zion. Their Babylonian captors apparently knew about the songs celebrating Zion as the dwelling place of God on earth and the boasting about Zion as an impregnable fortress (see Pss 46, 48, 76, 84, 122). But the Babylonians had conquered Zion and destroyed the Temple there. Their requests to hear the songs of Zion played and sung by the exiles were designed to mock the pretensions of the Judean exiles, to "rub it in" and remind them of their bitter defeat.

The psalmist's curse upon himself (137:4-6) follows his recognition that he cannot sing those songs of Zion during exile in a foreign land. That would be too painful. But not singing those songs does not mean that he will ever forget Jerusalem. He still regards Jerusalem as his "highest joy." His oath takes an "if . . . then" form, and is expressed in a chiastic (ABBA) pattern. He claims that if he ever forgets Jerusalem, he would want his right hand to wither and his tongue to cling to the roof of his mouth. These are symptoms of a stroke on the left side of the brain resulting in paralysis and atrophy of the right hand as well as aphasia. That would leave the psalmist unable to sing the songs of Zion or any other songs.

If Psalm 137 stopped with verse 6, it would be merely a poignant reflection on the misery of exile, with a small spark of hope for return to Zion. However, its final stanza consisting of two curses against Israel's enemies (137:7-9) has made it notorious. In the first curse (137:7) he asks God to "remember" (in the sense of exacting revenge upon) the Edomites, a people from the southeast of Judah, who played a part in destroying Jerusalem (see Lam 4:21; Ezek 25:12-14). The second curse (137:8-9) is against the Babylonians, who had the principal role in the destruction of Jerusalem and the subsequent exile. Here rather than calling on God to be the agent of vengeance, the psalmist pronounces two beatitudes ("happy shall they be") on those persons who exact retaliation against Babylon and even dash infants against rocks. It is quite possible that Babylonian soldiers had done such things to Judean children. And so this may be a matter of "an eye for eye."

Psalms 137 is full of raw emotions, including the cruel taunting of captives, an extravagant oath, and an egregious example of bloodthirsty revenge. Sometimes hope is not pretty. In the midst of this emotional cauldron there is a small spark of hope that the exiles might return home and again sing their songs of Zion. In fact, that hope was fulfilled in 537 B.C.E. when the Persian king Cyrus conquered Babylon and allowed the Judean exiles to return home and rebuild their temple to Yahweh (see Isa 40–55).

A similar mixture of raw emotions and a glimmer of hope appears in the New Testament book of Revelation. There John uses the terrible things said about Babylon in the Old Testament to describe what he hoped God might do to the Roman Empire and its allies. He also hoped that the risen Jesus would appear as the divine warrior and be the instrument of God's vengeance. His ultimate hope was eternal life with God and the Lamb in the New Jerusalem.

Questions: Where did the exiled community find its spark of hope? How do you explain the vengeful comments in verses 7-9? Is there sometimes a dark side to hope?

38. INCENSE (PSALM 141)

"Let my prayer be counted as incense before you,
and the lifting up of my hands as an evening sacrifice." (Ps 141:2)

Incense was part of the sacrificial rituals carried out in the Israelite tabernacle and later at the Jerusalem Temple. A recipe for the special kind of incense mixture to be used in these rites is preserved in Exodus 30:34-38. Special altars were set aside for burning the incense, and the priests were to offer "fragrant incense" every morning. Incense served the very practical purpose of off-setting the foul smells associated with the animal sacrifices. As Psalm 141:2 indicates, incense also came to be a symbol of prayer floating up to God in heaven.

Psalm 141 is an individual lament in which the complaints, petitions, and statements of trust in God are mixed together. However, at least a general outline can be discerned: address to God (141:1-2), petition (141:3-4), complaints (141:5-7), statement of trust (141:8), and petition (141:9-10). Although the image of prayer floating up to God like incense is soothing, the prayer itself in Psalm 141 arises out of an intense personal struggle in which the psalmist tries very hard to keep up his resolve and hope.

In the address to the Lord (141:1-2), the psalmist conveys the urgency of his prayer: "come quickly . . . give ear . . ." He compares his prayer to the incense offered in the morning at the Temple (Exod 30:7) and to the evening sacrifice (Exod 29:38-42). In the psalmist's historical context these images need not be interpreted as criticisms of material sacrifices. Like many Old

Testament writers, the psalmist here assumes the existence of material sacrifices and develops his analogies on that basis.

In the first petition (141:3-4), the psalmist asks God to help him overcome his own attraction to evildoing. He wants to "go straight" but recognizes that it will be a struggle to do so. He needs divine help to get control over his speech (141:3) and his heart (141:4). He knows that he must stay away from evil companions whose bad influence may corrupt him. His struggles sound much like what many alcoholics, drug addicts, and gang members go through today.

The "complaint" in verses 5-7 is more a resolution to willingly accept the discipline that the righteous and faithful may mete out to the psalmist if only he can escape the moral contamination that comes from associating with the wicked. His situation is like that envisioned in the image of the "two ways" in Psalm 1. He has chosen the way of the wise and righteous, but seems unsure of his ability to stay on that way. Meanwhile, he wishes and prays for the punishment and even the violent deaths of the wicked.

In his affirmation of trust in God (141:8), the psalmist hopes for security and stability in God as his only "refuge," and asks that God not leave him "defenseless." Again there are hints of the struggle still going on in the soul of the psalmist.

That struggle comes out again in the second petition (141:9-10). On the one hand, the psalmist prays that God will keep him away from the "trap" and "snares" set for him by evildoers. On the other hand, he asks that the wicked may fall into their own "nets" and that he alone may escape.

Despite its beautiful imagery, Psalm 141 is a tough prayer. Unlike many biblical laments where at the end the crisis seems to have been resolved and peace restored, here we do not know how the struggle turns out. The psalmist has intellectually chosen the right way but fears that on his own he will not be able to persevere. And so he seeks divine help in doing what he has to do to stay on the right way, and to avoid the attractions of bad companions. His "conversion" is still in process.

Unlike the psalmists, early Christians did develop the idea of prayer as a substitute for material sacrifices. The author of Hebrews urged his audience to "continually offer a sacrifice of praise to God" (13:15), which includes professions of faith and good works. Paul in Romans 12:1 exhorts Christians "to present your bodies as a living sacrifice, holy and acceptable to God." And 1 Peter 2:5 encourages the offering of "spiritual sacrifices acceptable to God through Jesus Christ." Early Christians were convinced that Jesus' death constituted the one perfect sacrifice for sins. Therefore they no longer offered material sacrifices like those carried out in the Jerusalem Temple. (See the letter to the Hebrews for the full theological rationale.)

Questions: How do you respond to the use of incense in liturgical rituals today? Do the psalmist's spiritual struggles correspond in any way to your own struggles? How do you understand the idea of "spiritual sacrifices"?

39. The God of Jacob (Psalm 146)

> *"Happy are those whose help is the God of Jacob,*
> *whose hope is in the Lord their God."* (Ps 146:5)

The Psalter ends with a block of five psalms (146–150) devoted to praising God. They appeal especially to God's mighty acts in creation and in Israel's early history. Connected with their praise of God is the conviction that the God who has done such marvels in the past can be trusted and relied upon in the future. From that perspective these psalms of praise are also songs of hope, and so they are a fitting conclusion to the book of Psalms as a book of hope.

Psalm 146 is a hymn of praise. It begins and ends with "Hallelujah," (again, translated in the NRSV as "Praise the Lord"), as do all of the five concluding hymns of praise. In verses 1-4 the psalmist first resolves to praise God and to hope in God alone. Then in verses 5-10 he pronounces a blessing on those who hope in God, and recounts the virtues of God or the characteristic ways in which the "God of Jacob" acts. Jacob's other name, of course, was Israel. Here the focus of praise, however, is not so much creation or Israel's early history as it is the character of the God of Jacob and why those in need can hope in him.

The psalmist's resolve to praise God (146:1-4) takes the form of a dialogue with himself ("O my soul"). He promises to praise God all during his life, and contrasts God as the ground of hope with what can be expected from human patrons. The main problem with human patrons is that they are mortal. With their passing, one's own hope dies with them. Not so with the God of Jacob!

The catalog of God's virtues in verses 5-10 takes the form of a beatitude: "Happy are those whose help is the God of Jacob, whose hope is in the LORD their God" (146:5). What kind of help can such persons expect? What can they hope for? The response to such questions takes the form of a list of phrases that describe Yahweh's typical ways of acting. While acknowledging God's work of creation, the psalmist focuses especially on God's special care for those who are most in need: the oppressed, hungry, imprisoned, blind, strangers, and orphans and widows. He loves the righteous and hates the wicked (146:8, 9).

What sets the God of Jacob apart from human patrons is that this God "keeps faith forever" (146:6). In the course of Psalm 146 the psalmist identifies the God of Jacob/Israel as the creator of heaven and earth (146:6) and as the one who makes his dwelling on Mount Zion (146:10). What makes the God of Jacob the only sure reason for trusting and hoping is that he "will reign forever . . . for all generations" (146:10).

According to Christian faith, the God of Jacob is the Father of Our Lord Jesus Christ. One of the most prominent themes in Jesus' teaching is trust in God as his heavenly Father. In Matthew 6:25-34 Jesus urges us not to be overly concerned with material matters but rather to consider how his heavenly Father cares for all his creatures, even the most apparently insignificant. According to Luke 23:46, Jesus, at the moment of his death, made his own the words of Psalm 31:5: "Father, into your hands I commend my spirit." The God of Jacob can be trusted because he is immortal. The God of Jacob is the God of hope. The God of hope is the God of Jesus.

Questions: Why is a song of praise also a song of hope? Why do you trust and hope in God? What are the implications of God's ways of acting for your ways of acting?

40. THE SOUND OF MUSIC (PSALM 150)

> *"Praise him with trumpet sound;*
> *praise him with lute and harp!"* (Ps 150:3)

Music is an essential component of Jewish and Christian worship. When a community sings well together, there is a strong sense of the union of hearts and minds. When the singing is accompanied by musical instruments, the celebration is all the more festive. Most of the compositions contained in the book of Psalms were originally intended to be sung, most likely with musical accompaniment. The most obvious setting for most psalms was the liturgical life of the Jerusalem Temple.

Psalm 150 is the fifth and last hymn of praise (146–150), and concludes the book of Psalms. It may even have been composed expressly to round off the Psalter. It begins and ends with "Hallelujah." It features ten imperatives that urge the praise of God, plus one final expansive directive ("let everything . . . praise"). The structure is most easily grasped with the help of four simple questions: Where? Why? How? and Who?

Where? In verse 1 the psalmist urges that God be praised in his "sanctuary" and in his "firmament." The sanctuary is most likely the Jerusalem Temple, though many interpreters take it to mean the heavenly sanctuary. The firmament is the sky, that is, the great space between the heavens and earth. The idea is that God should be praised everywhere in creation.

Why? In verse 2 the psalmist gives reasons why God should be praised. There are two main reasons: the mighty acts of God, and God's own intrinsic goodness. The mighty acts would surely include creation and the complex of events from the Exodus to the entrance into the Promised Land. These divine actions have been repeatedly celebrated throughout the book of Psalms.

How? According to verses 3-5, the Lord is be praised with full musical accompaniment. The list includes every musical instrument mentioned thus far in the book of Psalms. So we have (as it were) a symphony played by a full orchestra. Included in the list is mention of dance accompanied by the tambourine.

Who? Those expected to praise God are mentioned only in the final verse (150:6). It is everything that breathes, in heaven and on earth, on land and in the sea. All are invited to share in the grand chorus of praise to God.

It is likely that early Christians sang psalms (including many from the book of Psalms) in their worship services and other assemblies. There is also evidence in the New Testament that Christians composed hymns about Christ as the Servant of God (Phil 2:6-11), the Wisdom of God (Col 1:15-20), and the Word of God (John 1:1-18). An early second-century pagan observer, Pliny, who was the Roman governor of Bithynia in Asia Minor (present-day Turkey), noted that at their gatherings Christians customarily sang hymns to Christ "as to a god."

Most people today find good communal singing to be invigorating and uplifting. There is an old saying that whoever sings prays twice. The psalms in their Hebrew forms are used in various forms of Jewish worship. Many famous Christian hymns derive directly from compositions in the book of Psalms or are adaptations of them. In the current Catholic eucharistic liturgy there is a psalm assigned to every set of lectionary readings for both Sundays and weekdays. From Martin Luther's time onward, Protestants have developed a great tradition of communal hymn singing, with the biblical book of Psalms as a major source.

As we sing our hymns and play our musical instruments, we today are part of the grand chorus described in Psalm 150: "Let everything that breathes praise the Lord." That is what we hope for when we say with Jesus, "Thy kingdom come!"

Questions: How important is music to your participation in liturgical worship? Why is Psalm 150 an appropriate conclusion to the book of Psalms? What theological vision does it convey?

Epilogue

HOPE IN THE
BOOK OF PSALMS

Hope is a desire accompanied by the possibility of, or belief in, its realization. Hope has an object or focus, looks toward the future, and has a basis or ground in reality. As a theological virtue, hope has God as its origin, object, and ground.

Hope is a prominent theme in the book of Psalms. There the hopes of God's people are expressed in open and metaphorical language, with an abundant use of images. The psalms convey various aspects of hope, from abiding and waiting in hope, to struggling to persevere in hope, and even seeking vengeance on others. Thus they capture many of the dimensions present in our own experiences of hope.

The psalmists hope for release from sickness, sin, danger, and enemies, and seek refuge and security in and with God. Their hopes are oriented toward God as their shepherd, warrior, savior, and king, and to the institutions established by God for the people such as the Torah, kingship, the Jerusalem Temple, and material sacrifices. Their hopes are based largely on what God has done in creation and in the complex of events from the Exodus to the entrance into the Promised Land. While rich in theological insights, the psalms lack a clear vision of life after death and of the future kingdom of God.

In this volume I have tried to let the psalms speak for themselves by respecting their literary artistry, placing them in their ancient historical context, and clarifying their theological message. As a Catholic biblical scholar I have noted links between the Psalms and Jesus and the New Testament, in order to suggest how much in the book of Psalms points toward the paschal mystery of Jesus' life, death, and resurrection. I have also sought to encourage twenty-first-century readers to apply these ancient texts to their own lives today and so be better signs of hope in a world where it is in short supply.

My hope for this volume is that it may contribute to realizing in some small way the hope expressed by Paul in Romans 15:13: "May the God of hope fill you with all joy and peace in believing so that you may abound in hope by the power of the Holy Spirit."

FOR REFERENCE AND FURTHER STUDY

Anderson, Bernhard W. and Steven Bishop. *Out of the Depths: The Psalms Speak to Us Today*. Louisville: Westminster John Knox, 2000.

Attridge, Harold W. and Margot E. Fassler, eds. *Psalms in Community: Jewish and Christian Textual, Liturgical, and Artistic Traditions*. Atlanta: Society of Biblical Literature, 2003.

Brown, William P. *Seeing the Psalms: A Theology of Metaphor*. Louisville: Westminster John Knox, 2002.

Brueggemann, Walter. *The Message of the Psalms: A Theological Commentary*. Minneapolis: Augsburg, 1984.

Clifford, Richard J. *Psalms 1–72; Psalms 73–150*. Abingdon Old Testament Commentaries. Nashville: Abingdon, 2002–2003.

Flint, Peter W. and Patrick D. Miller, eds. *The Book of Psalms: Composition and Reception*. Leiden: Brill, 2003.

Gunkel, Hermann. *An Introduction to the Psalms: The Genres of the Religious Lyric of Israel*. Macon, GA: Mercer University Press, 1998.

Holladay, William. *The Psalms Through Three Thousand Years: Prayerbook of a Cloud of Witnesses*. Minneapolis: Augsburg, 1993.

Hossfeld, Frank-Lothar and Erich Zenger. *Psalms 2: A Commentary on Psalms 51–100*. Hermeneia. Minneapolis: Fortress, 2005.

Lohfink, Norbert. *In the Shadow of Your Wings: New Readings of Great Texts from the Bible*. Collegeville: Liturgical Press, 2003.

Mays, James L. *Preaching and Teaching the Psalms*. Louisville: Westminster John Knox, 2006.

Miller, Partrick D. *Interpreting the Psalms*. Philadelphia: Fortress, 1986.

Mowinckel, Sigmund. *The Psalms in Israel's Worship*. Nashville: Abingdon, 1967.

Moyise, Steve and Maarten J. J. Menken, eds. *The Psalms in the New Testament*. Edinburgh: T&T Clark, 2004.

Murphy, Roland E. *The Gift of the Psalms*. Peabody, MA: Hendrickson, 2000.

Pleins, J. David. *The Psalms: Songs of Tragedy, Hope, and Justice*. Maryknoll, NY: Orbis, 1993.

Schaefer, Konrad. *Psalms*. Berit Olam. Collegeville: The Liturgical Press, 2001.

Stec, David M. *The Targum of Psalms*. Collegeville: Liturgical Press, 2004.

Stuhlmueller, Carroll. *Psalms*. Old Testament Message. Wilmington, DE: Glazier, 1983.

Zenger, Erich. *A God of Vengeance? Understanding the Psalms of Divine Wrath*. Louisville: Westminster John Knox, 1996.

INDEX OF SUBJECTS

INDEX OF ANCIENT TEXTS

108   *Why Do We Hope?*